LEADERSHIP ELEMENTS:
A Guide to Building Trust

By Mike Mears

LEADERSHIP ELEMENTS:
A Guide to Building Trust

Acknowledgements

A special appreciation to all the CIA supervisors and managers who helped me refine my Periodic Table of the Leadership Elements over the years. And thanks to my family (Pat, Alissa, and Alex) for their patient on-call proofreading. Alton Johnson has an uncanny ability to take the cartoon locked in my mind and put it distinctly on paper. Finally, thanks to Barbara Brown for her incredibly long hours of editing and rewriting. Barbara is one of those rare people whose right and left-brain both function at high levels: she is as comfortable talking about element 95, Concern for Others, as she is with Element 81, Use Pareto Charts. Her flair for graphics and design helped highlight many of the key elements.

Table of Contents

Introduction

TEN YEARS AGO, A TOP CIA EXECUTIVE ASKED ME WHY THE ORGANIZATIONAL BOTTOM WAS SO FREQUENTLY DISCONNECTED FROM THE TOP. It was a question that changed my life as I launched a journey to find the answer. I thought back to my eight years of doing turnarounds and private equity investing for General Electric and my experiences running a combat platoon, a nuclear missile site, and public sector entities. I was struck by the leadership commonalities in these very different settings.

Later, when CIA Director George Tenet asked me to start up and manage the CIA's Leadership Academy, I noticed that even good leaders throughout the agency experienced startling revelations about basic aspects of leadership during the training. My goal was to compile and organize a compendium of management and leadership concepts for all types of organizations, creating not just another management book but a set of easy-to-remember principles organized by concept. I was striving to create a concise, organized family of concepts—a Periodic Table of the Elements of Leadership and Management.

I experienced firsthand the forgettable simplicity of its basic elements: I frequently forgot to thank well-performing employees. Didn't they know they were doing a great job? As a leadership element, Say thanks (element 28) sounds trite, but we'll see in a moment that it actually affects the brain chemistry of the recipient. When I forgot to use it, and say, thanks, I frittered away potential employee performance.

I noticed this same propensity often in public and private-sector managers to either forget the basics or not combine the basics in effective ways. I spent weekends cobbling together the Periodic Table of the Elements of Leadership and Management, mostly as a joke. When I presented it at CIA Leadership Academy graduations, I was surprised and pleased that it generated rich discussions among attendees. The same thing occurred when I used it as a gift at public speaking events. The chart was a leadership practice field and provided people with a safe way to thrash out thorny workplace issues.

The magic of what you see when you unfold the Periodic Table of the Elements of Leadership and Management is not the solitary elements but how they can group together in compounds to make people's lives better while driving increasingly better performance.

When you mix the elements into compounds, you get startling results. For example, by itself, element 74 (Accountability) can be highly toxic, but it becomes beneficently stable when combined with element 108 (Define outcomes). By the way, part of the answer to the CIA executive's question about the disconnect between the top and bottom of organizations may be an imbalance between those two elements.

In my own case, I glance at the chart for five minutes every morning to remember to do things that don't come naturally to me, like saying thank you. As one of my students once said, "Leadership isn't rocket science. It's more complicated!" What he meant is that the elements are individually simple, but how you mix them and actually put them into practice correctly is extraordinarily challenging.

Some of the elements are so overused they've become discredited. For example, "Have character," "Wander around," and "Brainstorm" seem hackneyed. But study them closely—some of them pack twists and surprises or become explosive, even nuclear, when mixed with other elements. At first glance, some seem too closely related, like Humor (element 1) and Play (element 25), but they sport important differences.

How the Chart is Organized to Help You

As we progress through the book, you may wonder why the atomic weight numbers are not listed in order. If we covered the elements in numerical order, we would march from the easiest (lightest) element to the hardest (heaviest), and it wouldn't be as helpful as talking about them within their natural groups, which are organized in columns. That's why group one consists of elements 1, 3, 11, 19, and so on. They all explain Know Yourself in a way Socrates would be proud of.

In CIA fashion, there are a few secret tricks and hidden relationships scattered throughout the chart for you to discover. I'll disclose one of them at the end of the book, but there are some undiscovered elements I'll leave for you to detect, develop, draw upon, and share with others. Some of the elements are certainly more important than others.

For example, when elements 90 (Provide fair and frequent feedback), 48 (Get employees involved), and 116 (Selection) are initiated in a much more rigorous and professional fashion than usual for organizations, they can have disproportionately positive effects on people and, therefore, on organizations. These, and a handful of other elements, rank in importance to oxygen and carbon found on the real periodic table; they can be combined in almost limitless ways with other elements to increase employee satisfaction and performance.

How the Book is Organized to Help You

Following this introduction is the entire Periodic Table of the Elements of Leadership and Management. We'll start by studying each element individually. Then, as in the real periodic table, we'll combine individual elements into twenty, powerful and meaningful groupings. Next, we'll clump the groups together into three massive families—Inspire, Improve, and Implement—which are the essence of great management and leadership. By properly balancing Inspire, Improve, and Implement, you produce high levels of organizational trust and productivity.

Note that the leadership elements fall on the left side of the chart while the management elements are on the right side—pure leadership involves inspiring, and pure management involves implementing. The overlap of good management and leadership—improvement—is a critical area. We'll see why in a moment.

When it comes to your own leadership competence, how others perceive your practice of the elements is important. Some leaders combine powerful elements into a leadership philosophy and feel they have it mastered; however, followers can misinterpret their actions and take away a completely wrong message. This frequently happens in the workplace and causes leaders and followers to blindly bump into and bruise one another throughout the day.

The good news is that implementing just a few of the elements you normally tend to overlook will improve your leadership and management. When it comes to leadership, perception is reality. To start, we'll take Socrates' advice and explore the first seven leadership elements clumped in a family called Know Yourself.

To get a full page color copy of the Periodic Table of the Elements of Leadership and Management go to http://mikemears.biz/Home_Page.

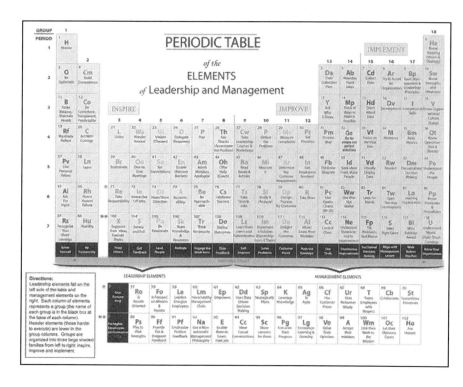

Inspire

Introduction

A leader inspires. When you are in the presence of an inspiring leader, you feel their energy and share their vision.

There is a groundswell of support and a shared belief around an inspiring leader. Inspired people want to take action. They want to make a vision reality. They are committed. They are passionate, and they want to rally others.

Business Week Online Communication (http://www.babsoninsight.com, October 10, 2007) author Carmine Gallo, a Pleasanton, California communications coach and author of the book, *Fire Them Up!* (John Wiley & Sons; October, 2007) offered a concise description of an inspiring leader. In her article she listed seven characteristics of inspiring leaders summarized below:

1. Demonstrate enthusiasm—Inspiring leaders have an abundance of passion for what they do.
2. Articulate a compelling course of action. Inspiring leaders craft and deliver a specific, consistent, and memorable vision.
3. Sell the benefit—an inspiring leader convinces people that it's about them. Inspiring leaders answer the question, "what's in this for me?"
4. Inspiring leaders tell stories. No amount of data can replace a story that people can relate to in their own lives.

5. Invite participation — Inspiring leaders get people involved. They know that employees want more than a paycheck. They want to know that their input is considered and their contributions are valuable in the big picture.

6. Are optimistic. Inspirational leaders believe in the future. They are able to paint a vivid picture of a different and better reality.

7. Encourage potential — Inspiring leaders help people believe in themselves. Inspiring leaders praise people and invest in them emotionally.

This list tracks leadership attributes described and targeted by leading talent selection and assessment companies, aligns with the Emotional Intelligence (EQ) work done by Daniel Goldman and others, and reflects the thoughts in most leadership books written over the last twenty-five years. More important, it probably matches what you *feel* are the appropriate leadership characteristics.

A politician, a minister, a family friend, or a teacher may have particularly inspired you. Remembering back to that time and to those events, do you recall which characteristics caused you to reflect on and perhaps change the direction of your life? Those are the characteristics of an inspiring leader.

Martin Luther King, Ronald Reagan, Winston Churchill, Oprah Winfrey, and Bill Gates are good example of inspiring leaders, but there are thousands more, unknown to most of us, with no official recognition, quietly inspiring their employees and co-workers.

My most inspiring leader was Secretary of Commerce Malcolm Baldrige. He was an extraordinarily competent leader yet full of humility. He was also a professional rodeo rider on the side, and I remember him sauntering around his office in jeans with a big bandana flopping out his back pocket. When he walked into the Department of Commerce cafeteria, employees would back off a bit — he was a cabinet secretary, after all — but Baldrige would wave them to him and say, "C'mon, c'mon, sit down and have lunch with me. Tell me what you're up to." He chatted with employees about whatever they were comfortable with—their jobs, hobbies, likes, dislikes, and even dreams. He captured the workforce with symbolic actions like these.

In 1987, when I was his representative in Moscow, I received an urgent cable at the American embassy. The message reported Mac Baldrige had died in a freak rodeo accident. It was the day the Commerce Department cried.

Recently, my wife, Pat, had a meeting with a group of Commerce Department employees. She rushed home to tell me, "You won't believe this, but over twenty years later, they're still talking about Mac Baldrige!" Great leaders inspire us that way.

You can be an inspiring leader, like Mac Baldrige, in your organization. The eight chapters in section 1 help you gain the insight and skills necessary to be an inspiring leader. You'll first learn about the essential need to know yourself—your strengths and weaknesses and how others might misperceive you. Next, you'll learn about the need for trust—be trustworthy and trust others. Trust is leadership's underlying foundation. You'll learn the importance of giving and receiving feedback as part of an overall strategy to engage, motivate, and lead people. Each chapter provides a discussion of individual elements that make up the required inspirational skills, as well as practice exercises. You may read the chapter in its entirety at one time or read one element a day. I hope you reflect on each element and discuss it with your team. Section 1 gives you practical advice and suggestions on how to become an inspiring leader.

Chapter 1: Know Yourself

Knowing yourself is one of the most challenging and important tasks of your life. If you know what you believe in, what you value, and how you define truth and beauty, you will be in a better position to understand what you want. You will also be empowered to achieve your goals both in business and in life.

Sun Tzu, in *The Art of War*, said, "Know the enemy and know yourself; in a hundred battles you will never be in peril." Knowing yourself helps you make good decisions, carry out actions effectively, and motivate your followers. Knowing yourself is also the path to knowing others, appreciating their strengths, and accepting their shortcomings.

You get to know yourself by reflecting on your beliefs, values, and experiences. You come to understand how others perceive you by asking for their feedback. In this chapter, we'll look at some common characteristics of how effective leaders and managers get to know themselves and how they return those lessons to others.

Leaders use humor
- It can help you make a point
- It can diffuse a situation

Leaders are optimists
- Optimists believe problems can be solved
- Employees prefer to be led by an optimist

Leaders know how to balance work and life
- They balance their own lives and jobs
- They recognize that their employees must have balance in their lives

Leaders take time to reflect

Leaders live their values

Leaders ask for input from peers, staff, and customers

Leaders know that they are not perfect

H

Humor

Humor plays a serious role in your communication with other people. Humor can be used to make a point or to diffuse a situation. When used about yourself, humor demonstrates your humility and can sometimes disarm a difficult situation. Before we discuss using humor, it is important to understand that humor in a business setting is *not* telling jokes — unless there is a business point being made. Humor is not mean-spirited. It is not making fun of a person or group, and it is not school yard use of forbidden words. Humor is a powerful tool that aids communication and fosters understanding.

Primary rule: Use humor about situations and not people unless the person is you. The types of humor that may work well in a business setting include anecdotes, situational humor, animal stories that serve as training metaphors, and acknowledgement of absurdities or contradictions in practice. According to Professor Jeffery Goldstein of Temple University, "people who use more humor tend to wield more influence over group decisions. Good, effective leaders combine communications and persuasion skills with an appropriate touch of humor to get their message across and to win support for their ideas."[ii]

Tip: *If you do not find yourself laughable, others will.*

O

Be optimistic

If you realized how powerful your thoughts are, you would never think a negative thought.
—Peace Pilgrim

Effective leaders are optimistic. They are optimistic and confident by nature, and they are able to convey their optimism to others in ways that are motivating — this is not Pollyanna optimism but a strong belief in their vision and their ability to make it happen. The optimism of a leader is founded in reality. Optimistic leaders focus on solving problems not on complaining or making excuses.

People can view the implications of events in different ways. An optimist sees the positive and attempts to capitalize on each possibility. Optimistic leaders are more resilient when things are not going well because they believe things will work out for the best. The optimistic leader believes that negative events are transitional, not permanent conditions. Optimistic leaders do not assume that a negative outcome foretells all future happenings.

Your employees prefer to be led by an optimist. They want to follow someone who keeps going and keeps them going in order to work through downturns in the natural business cycle. It is disturbing and de-motivating to have your manager constantly harping on what's wrong, what bad things are going to happen, and how helpless you are in the face of such conditions.

Being optimistic is also better for your health too. Optimistic people experience less stress and stress-related illnesses than pessimists. If you lean toward a pessimistic world view, here is good news: you can learn to be more optimistic. In his book, *Learned Optimism: How to Change Your Mind and Your Life,* Martin Seligman describes how to feel more positive and experience less stress in a research-supported approach called "learned optimism." Likewise, Susan Vaughn, in her book *Half Empty, Half Full: Understanding the Psychological Roots of Optimism,* applies both self-help and psychology to explain how we learn to be pessimists and how we can learn to be optimists.

11

B

Strike balance— maintain health

Your work life and your home life are both important to you, but in the frenetic pace of projects, plans, dealing with problems and competition, fighting traffic, and getting everything done at work, it is easy for life to get out of whack. You find yourself in the position of working on the squeakiest wheels and putting everything else off. This is not healthy, nor is it an effective strategy in the long run for either you or your organization.

The goal of maintaining a balance is not to change your task location from working at work to working at home. Achieving a balance means spending time with people who are important to you and doing activities you enjoy. Your goals should be to relieve stress, refresh your view of the world, and feed your spirit. The old adage "take time to smell the roses" is really a prescription for maintaining emotional and physical health. If you wonder how you are doing in maintaining balance, check out the Quint Careers Quiz on work–life balance (see the web link listed in the Further Reading section).

You also need to be sensitive to the work–life balance for your staff. Again, this consideration is not just humanitarian. It is in the best interest of the organization to have employees who achieve balance in their own lives as they will be healthier, happier, and more productive. Poor balance in your employees' lives may be demonstrated by poor attendance, excessive use of sick days, and poor employee retention—all of which cost the organization. Here are a few organizational attitudes and procedures you should consider offering to help your employees strike a healthy balance:

- Flextime—when possible, offer flexible hours, such as when work starts, hours worked, or days worked.
- Mental health days—these are like sick days except your employee is not sick; they just need to refresh.
- Telecommuting—increases and employees report greater job satisfaction when allowed to telecommute. Now, not all jobs can be done remotely, and not everyone is more productive when not at the office. However, selectively offering this can help employees balance their work–home life and reduce the added stress of commuting.
- Classes—offer lunchtime or after-work classes that promote stress reduction and relaxation.
- Consideration—be flexible in considering what it means to be an employee. If what you want is to get the job done, be open to ideas about job sharing and part-time workers.
- Communication—ask your employees; they may have some great, innovative ideas on reducing stress and achieving a balance in their lives.
- Leadership—take the lead in demonstrating a commitment to a work–life balance.

Balance is essential

19

<u>Rf</u>

Routinely reflect

Reflection is a calm and calming process that can also spur creativity. Reflection involves thinking through situations and events without the distractions that were likely present when the events were occurring. The goal of reflection is understanding and improvement.

Mr. Hyde Routinely Reflects

Of course, you don't want to deceive yourself like our friend Mr. Hyde, who saw himself reflected as kindly Dr. Jekyll. However, mirrored reflection can be helpful. Remember Perseus, who would have turned to stone had he looked directly at the hideous Medusa? He was able to slay her by looking at her reflection in a mirror.

Some leaders practice reflection by setting aside free time, like a Saturday morning, or while on airplanes, jogging, relaxing in a quiet place, or even in the shower. Others may actually get away from it all to a place that promotes quiet, reflective thought.

Reflection is a skill that involves observation, asking questions, and putting facts, ideas, and experiences together. You may find your reflection facilitated by writing down your thoughts. Here are some questions you should ask during your period of reflection:

- What was the sequence of events?
- What actions worked? Why did they work?
- What actions did not seem to work? Why?
- Does this situation remind me (us) of any other series of events or situations? How are they similar, and how are they different?
- Did I (we) learn anything from the experience?
- What can I (we) do differently next time?
- What did I (we) enjoy about this event? What didn't I (we) like?

37

Pv

Live personal values

A value is a belief or philosophy that underlies our worldview and the way we treat our family, employees, the community, and the environment. Values may be deep-seated, such as our view of the importance of empathy and our responsibility in determining right from wrong, or more superficial, such as the value we place on punctuality or ease of use. There are a few value topics listed below. The relative importance you place on these concepts influences your behavior as a manager and leader.

This list is much longer than the examples, but from it, you can gain the idea that personal values drive your actions and decisions. As a leader, you should act in concert with your values. However, be aware that others, including your employees, will view your actions through the filter of their own values. So while you may believe that you are being assertive in stating your point of view, others may see your behavior as aggressive and pushy. You may believe you are being tolerant and open-minded, whereas others think you are being indecisive.

It is important, in some cases, that your underlying values be understood by your employees because your personal values also reflect on the organization's values. You can accomplish some consonance by providing an explanation of your recommendations and decisions, which are founded on your personal values. You should also solicit feedback, formal and informal, which will indicate when your personal values are perhaps being misperceived.

Examples of Personal Values Topics		
Accountability	Achievement	Commitment
Competence	Collaboration	Courage
Equality	Fairness	Hard work
Honesty	Humility	Integrity
Justice	Reflection	Respect
Responsibility	Security	Study

55

Ai

Ask for input

These people have information that will help you be a better leader and manager:

- *Peers*
- *Employees*
- *Customers*
- *Bosses*
- *Spouse*
- *Friends*
- *Vendors*

Hint: The more subordinate brains you engage, the more successful you'll be. It's up to you to get the ball rolling by asking questions, then listening!

No one knows everything, and you're not expected to know everything, but as a leader, you're expected to *find* the answers. That's where input is essential. Other people have new ideas, different approaches to solving a problem, pieces of data you don't have, or helpful observations. The problem is they may not tell you what they know or think until you ask.

There are additional benefits to asking for input. Not only will you get different ideas, but your employees will feel more valuable and more a part of the solution and the organization. They'll respect you for asking. It's a win–win situation. Asking for input requires that you listen with an open mind, of course. Nothing will stop a person from giving you their input faster than penalizing them for doing so.

Penalizing is a harsh word, and most of the time, we do it inadvertently. We're rushed and keep typing—they think we're ignoring them. We give reasons it can't be done—they think we're closed to new ideas. We unconsciously act defensively—they are offended. In the other periodic table, when you throw cold water on cesium (element 55), it's highly explosive. Inadvertently closing down future input—our element 55—can be just as dangerous.

There are many effective ways to ask for input. You can implement an open-door policy and encourage employees to approach you with information or concerns. You can wander through the workplace (element 22) and ask questions or conduct employee surveys. You can also ask for feedback through e-mail.

Over time, you'll find that the input you receive is so useful that you may even choose to ask for input from people outside your organization. Peers in similar businesses are confronting many of the same challenges as you, and even in different types of organizations, there are those who deal with comparable problems and opportunities. People feel good about being asked for their opinions and observations. Do yourself a favor and ask for them.

A shortcoming seems like a bad thing—a character flaw, perhaps. "Short" before a word means inadequate—shortsighted, short-lived, short shrift. However, there is another way to think of shortcomings: they are the natural complement to your skills. For example, as a leader, you have a vision or a view of the way the future could be. You see further down the road than many people. That may mean you do not relish details—you do not dwell on the weeds along the path. So not being detail oriented may lead to skipping steps or moving too quickly. That is a shortcoming.

Our shortcomings are the eyes with which we see the ideal.
—Nietzsche

Rather than hide your shortcomings, you should recognize them and then work around them through other people and processes. You probably know some of your shortcomings because the world has given you feedback about them. You did well in school in thought classes like history, but you did badly in detail classes like accounting. Your mother reminded you frequently of your failures to pick up your clothes or be on time. As a leader and manager, you should reflect (element 19) on those shortcomings that interfere with your job execution.

When you realize a shortcoming, you can protect yourself and the organization by involving others who possess complementary skills. Using the skills of others for the greater good is the mark of a good manager and leader. If you fail to recognize your shortcomings and take a proactive approach, you risk failing and having your adversaries take advantage of your shortcomings. When you recognize and acknowledge your shortcomings and ask for help, others feel needed and valuable. They become part of the solution.

Eleanor Roosevelt was the wife of U.S. President Franklin D. Roosevelt. In many ways, she was a pioneer. She was the first woman to speak in front of a national convention and the first woman to have a syndicated column and to earn money through lectures. But in her youth, Eleanor was plagued by shyness and insecurity that could have kept her from speaking out and working for causes she believed in. Eleanor worked hard to overcome her natural shyness. She said, "You gain strength, courage and confidence by every experience in which you really stop to look fear in the face. You are able to say to yourself, I have lived through this horror. I can take the next thing that comes along."[iii]

EXERCISES

Use the personal values listed in element 37

Exercise 1
Value Behaviors

Select three value topics and list what each value means to you. How does your behavior reflect that value?

1. _____
   _____
   _____

2. _____
   _____
   _____

3. _____
   _____
   _____

Exercise 2
Shortcomings

Pick two behaviors you consider shortcomings. For each one, describe how you know about it and what you do to lessen its impact.

Improve Your Shortcomings

Shortcoming	Who told you	How do you lessen impact
(example)		
Don't listen well	*Spouse*	*Repeat what I heard*
1)		
2)		

Chapter 2: Be Trustworthy

Introduction:
Being trustworthy is more than a desirable characteristic of leadership and management—it is an *essential* characteristic. If you aren't trustworthy, employees and customers won't feel they can count on you when the going is tough, nor will they give you honest information or opinions.

You are perceived as trustworthy when your actions are consistent. You do the right things regardless of personal risk. Trustworthy people keep promises. Trustworthy people show that they are concerned about the interests and well-being of others. People trust based on their observations of how you behave and treat them.

Steve Marr, CEO of a large U.S. import–export company writes on his blog, *Business Proverbs*[iv], that "Genuinely trustworthy leaders embrace and demonstrate four basic behaviors: (1) follow-through, (2) readily admitting mistakes, (3) sharing decision making with others, and (4) accepting responsibility for one's own actions and results."

What you will learn in this chapter:

Building competence
- Making the effort
- Using listening, observation, and reflection

Leaders are consistent
- Your behavior should match your words
- Use feedback to gage your consistency

Leaders act with courage
- For themselves
- For their employees

Leaders take time to learn
- Why learning never stops
- What is your best learning style

Leaders recognize and accept their failures
- Why you should acknowledge honest failures
- How to apply lessons learned from failure

Leaders are humble about their gifts and accomplishments
- Recognize the contributions of others
- Work for the organization not for you own grandeur

4

Cm

Build competence

Learn from your successes

Learn from your failures

Practice

Measure

Keep trying

Competence is doing things well, repeatedly. Competence requires study, practice, and reflection. There are many skills in which you need to be competent as a manager and leader. Effective communicating, decision making, planning, organizing, motivating, conflict managing, and problem solving are but a few of them. *Leadership & Life a Guide to Building Trust* provides you with a compendium of these desired competencies.

Although the task of building competence across so many diverse skill sets may seem daunting, self study is a great beginning. By applying the techniques discussed below, you will continue to build and improve your competence with your life's experiences.

Of course, just living through an experience doesn't automatically lead to competence in similar activities. Rather than letting experiences simply flow over them, exceptional leaders and managers strive to extract useful lessons that can be applied in similar circumstances. Great leaders learn from others and share what they have learned to help others become more competent. Few activities reinforce your competence more than teaching others.

Steps to Build Competence

- Learn from experience. Always try to do a task better. Watch others — copy success and avoid strategies that fail.
- Study — read what others have recommended about the task area.
- Seek experiences that will increase your competence in required areas.
- Practice, practice, practice.
- Find a mentor — someone with competence in the skills you want to acquire.
- Solicit and welcome feedback to hone your skills.
- Reflect — what is happening, what did happen, what worked, what did not work, how could the outcome be improved, and what should I have known when I started?
- Listen — passive learning is still learning and helps you avoid repeating others' failing strategies and emulate successful ones.
- Facilitate building competence in your staff and organization.
- Use feedback to constantly improve your performance and that of the organization or project.
- Reward competence in others.

12

Co

Be consistent, transparent, and predictable

Good parents and good leaders have much in common. In fact, we'll later see how one whole family of elements applies to raising teenagers! Applying consistency in your expectations, administration of rules, and allocation of rewards gives your employees (and children) security because they know what to expect. Of course, as the prisoner cartoon shows, you can go overboard applying any element.

Inconsistent expectations have the opposite effect of consistent ones. Until your employees know what is expected or how you will respond to their behavior, they are rudderless. Your inconsistent behaviors create anxiety. Being consistent and predictable not only provides security for employees, it helps build trust. This is true with customers and stakeholders too.

There must be consistency in direction.[v]
—W. Edward Deming

Transparency reinforces a leader's consistency and predictability. Transparency means that employees and other stakeholders can see and understand the reasons for your expectations and behavior. Transparency can be tricky. It includes conscious actions, like what you say, but it also includes automatic or unconscious actions. For example, if you say you have an open-door policy but greet employees with a frown on your face, you are sending a mixed signal. You negate your words with unconscious actions. Being transparent means that your behaviors and your words are consistent in the minds of others.

Predictability reinforces expectations and will help develop positive behavior patterns.

Consistency, reliability, and predictability are the cornerstones of solid, long-term relationships with customers and employees. To retain your customer and employee base and the loyalty of both, strive for transparency in your decisions and consistency in your quality.

Are you being consistent? Get feedback!

You are not always the best judge of how your behavior is perceived. You want to be consistent, predictable, and transparent, and you believe you are, but feedback is the way you verify that belief. If you are getting inconsistent behaviors from your employees, they may be reflecting the inconsistent behavior in you. Check it out. This is so important, one whole family of elements is devoted to getting feedback.

Guidelines for Consistency, Predictability, and Transparency

- Don't have different reactions to the same behaviors depending on whose behavior it is or when it happens.
- Don't commit to doing something you cannot or will not do.
- Do what you say you will do. (Be cautious here: employees will often seize upon and remember a promise or hint you made but long ago forgot.)
- Be aware of your nonverbal behavior (body language) and strive to make sure it is consistent with your words.
- If some processes or rules are not applied to everyone, be transparent and explain why.
- Ensure that high-level goals, such as the organization's mission and vision, are consistently applied across the organization.
- If it has been brought to your attention that you are being inconsistent, consider it, and, if it is true, provide feedback on why or offer an apology. (As we will later see in element 43, admitting mistakes often separates great from average leaders.)
- Forgive yourself. Even when you try to be consistent, predictable, and transparent, there will be times when you fail. You are only human. Accept it and move on.

Yeah, personal security's a real plus, but I love the predictability:
the rules, the schedule, the water, the bread....

C

Act with courage

We are taught to understand, correctly, that courage is not the absence of fear, but the capacity for action despite our fears.[vi]
—*Senator John McCain*

There is a certain degree of satisfaction in having the courage to admit one's errors. It not only clears up the air of guilt and defensiveness, but often helps solve the problem created by the error.[vii]
—*Dale Carnegie*

Physical courage allows you to act in the face of pain, hardship, or threat of death. Shepherding your career rarely requires physical courage, although it may as you can see from the example at the end of this element. However, moral courage is quite another thing. It is very likely in your career that you will face opportunities to act with moral courage. You display moral courage when you take actions that you believe are correct but place you in risk of losing support, respect, and perhaps even your job. "Moral courage means...overcoming the fear of shame and humiliation in order to admit one's mistakes, to confess a wrong, to reject evil conformity, to denounce injustice, and also to defy immoral or imprudent orders," says William Ian Miller, author of *The Mystery of Courage*. A courageous act may be judged favorably by history, but at the time you are compelled to take action, you do so with no guarantee of favorable acceptance.

History is replete with examples of individuals who acted with courage. There are stories of people in extreme circumstances making the decision to put life, limb, and careers on the line in the name of doing what they believed was the right thing to do for the greater good. However, you do not need to be a president, a senator, or a general to have opportunities to act with courage. As a manager and leader in any size organization, there are circumstances you will confront where you can choose to act with courage. Some examples of managing and leading with courage are provided by Ray Weekes's example in his article, "Wanted: Leaders with Courage." According to Weekes, "Courage for a business leader can be confronting employees directly affected by your downsizing decisions and making yourself vulnerable to their criticisms and anger. Courage is caring enough about your values that you uphold them in the face of risks. Leadership is about change and it takes real courage, at times, to maintain your resolve when the risks of change become blindingly apparent."

Acting with courage sometimes means violating norms or organizational culture—something others will resist. Remember, the people opposing you are good people; they just believe you are stepping out too far or taking a risk that could harm the organization. Have patience and keep communications open with them. Here are a few examples of courageous management and leadership behaviors derived from the Periodic Table of Elements of Leadership and Management.

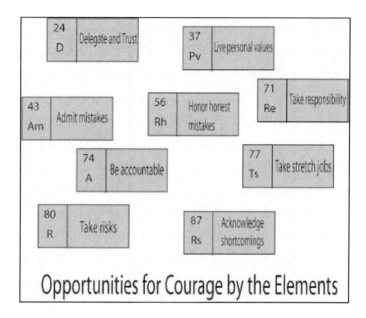

Opportunities for Courage by the Elements

A case in point: **Alayne Gentul**

The director of human resources at Fiduciary Trust, Alayne was 44 and married with two children. Alayne was a victim and hero during the 9/11 bombings. With the help of other staff, including Ed Emery, Alayne managed to save at least 40 colleagues by encouraging people to leave the South Tower as soon as she heard what had happened to the North Tower (the first one to be hit). It was with this in mind that Alayne went up to the 97th floor to try and find more people who might not be aware of the seriousness of the situation.[viii]

56	Failure in the corporate world means not being where you said you would be when you said you would to be there. Your team may miss a deadline. A product may not meet expectations. A new procedure has unintended and undesirable consequences. A contract is awarded to a competitor. Admitting failure and accepting responsibility is the first and essential step in moving onward to success. To be effective, admitting failure must happen quickly, with an honest appraisal of what happened and why.
Rh	
Honor honest failure	

Johnson & Johnson provided a classic example in 1982 when they immediately halted production and marketing and removed all Tylenol from retail shelves after discovering product tampering in Chicago. It cost the company over 100 million dollars, yet the chairman said it was an easy decision since the company's central value of consumer safety trumped profit making. Honoring the failure made the company trustworthy in customers' eyes.

Honoring honest failure means taking responsibility for your errors of omission and commission. Ignoring failure, pretending that everything is going according to plan, or looking for a scapegoat may do you and your organization irreparable harm. When you accept an honest failure, you provide the impetus to improve or fix a situation, and you also accomplish something that will help your organization in the future—you set an example of the expectation of honesty that your employees will emulate. On the other hand, not honoring honest failure sends a subtle message to employees that may lead to cover-ups, lying, or organizational stagnation.

Honoring Honest Failure

- To honor honest failure, first recognize you are failing.
- Get the facts—what, when, how, and why.
- Decide whom to tell and how to provide the information as soon as possible.
- Acknowledge the failure and take responsibility for your part.
- If possible, develop a plan to reach the original goal a different way or correct the consequences.
- Learn and move on.

A case in point: The following is from an interview with Herb Kelleher, executive chairman and cofounder of Southwest Airlines, by *Babson Insights*[x], October 2004: "I'll just give you an illustration. Some years ago our pilots got into a tough situation, and I didn't realize how serious it was. It had reached the point where it was becoming a little fight with the FAA, not over safety issues, but it was becoming a competitive issue. At first I didn't realize the heat that was being brought on our pilots, so I was saying, 'Don't pay any attention to this nonsense.' Then after looking more closely I saw their problem, so I got all the pilots together and said, 'I made a hell of a mistake, and it's costing you.'" Southwest then worked with the FAA to solve the problem and reimburse the pilots.

Hu

Humility

Humility is an attribute of truly great leaders according to Jim Collins in his book *Good to Great* and in his classic article for *Harvard Business Review*, "Level 5 Leadership: The Triumph of Humility and Fierce Resolve." Humility is more than just being nice; humility means understanding no person acting alone can create a great organization and that every employee is needed in the effort.

Humility is the opposite of arrogance, pride, and haughtiness and keeps ego and arrogance from getting in the way of realistic appraisals and good decisions. It is not to be confused with self-deprecation. A telling quote that embodies the attitude of humility comes from Sir Isaac Newton—arguably one of the most accomplished scientists in history—in his letter to fellow scientist Robert Hooke: "If I have seen further it is by standing on the shoulders of giants."

Humble leaders motivate others by understanding and signaling the importance of others' contributions. He or she serves as a role model for an organization. Humble leaders aren't milquetoast; they have strong drive. Dan Baker explains this in his insightful book, *What Happy Companies Know*: "Humble leaders have powerful egos, meaning appropriate self-esteem as opposed to an overinflated self-opinion. They are demanding, but driving their demands is a capacity for caring and a desire to help others excel, rather than a desire for personal domination."

Historical examples of humble leaders include Jesus, Buddha, Gandhi, and Cinncinatus. Cincinnatus was plucked from his field by a senatorial delegation informing him he had been chosen to be dictator to save Rome. In spite of the personal hardship, he donned his senatorial toga, called up an army, beat the troublesome Aequi, resigned as dictator, and returned to his farm all within sixteen days!

Colin Powell is a modern day example of humility. Powell was modest even as a four star general. To remind himself to avoid the self-importance trap, he kept a sign above his desk with Lincoln's Civil War comment, "I can make more generals, but horses cost money." Powell knew the troops and junior officers did the army's real work. He was humble.

EXERCISES

Exercise 1
Change

Being a change agent requires learning, consistency and courage.

Your industry is poised for major changes in production quality control because of international competition and new legislation. You need to change processes that have been in place for thirty years and everyone is comfortable with. You anticipate resistance and maybe even an employee revolt. List the actions you would take to instruct, get buy-in, and deal with resistance, including possibly terminating employees.

List the actions you would take to be an effective change agent.

1. _____
   _____
   _____

2. _____
   _____
   _____

3. _____
   _____
   _____

4. _____
   _____
   _____

Exercise 2
Honest Failure

Pick two examples of honest failure in your work or personal life. For each, identify how the failure was acknowledged and what you learned.

Learning from Failure

Instance of honest failure	What did you do?	What did you learn?
1)		
2)		

Chapter 3: Trust Others

Trusting others can be frightening because you give up the illusion of control over outcomes. To gain increased productivity that comes from working with people who are invested in your organization and its future and in solving the challenges to be successful, it is essential that you learn to trust others. One clear advantage to trusting others is you are then perceived as trustworthy.

Trusting others is based on the expectation that the trustee will perform an action that serves your common goals. Reciprocity is the key to this family of elements as well as the previous one. Be trustworthy. People resist being influenced by leaders they don't trust or who don't trust them. People sense how you feel about them. If you want your employees to trust you and trust one another, you have to take the first step and trust them. Below are a few of the responses to what employees seek from leaders and business organizations, based on a survey[xiii] by Jeff Magee, PhD., publisher of *Performance Magazine*:

- Knowing that they are appreciated via regular feedback from both their immediate manager-leader and the organization.
- Tangible evidence of their ideas being sought, considered, and occasionally acted upon.
- Trusting in them to do their assigned work and avoid micro management intervention.
- They can trust that the leaders don't lie, mislead or act in self-serving manners.

Learn to listen
- Listening to your employees
- Using feedback to improve listening

Brainstorming
- Helping your group be effective at brainstorming
- Conducting a brainstorming meeting

Leaders take responsibility
- For their actions and outcomes
- Even in the little things

Leaders know when to let others' ideas have a voice
- How keeping a low profile helps creativity
- Trusting that employees can generate great ideas

L

Listen

As a manager and leader within your organization, one of the most useful skills you can develop is the ability to listen. Listen to ideas, concerns, and complaints from your employees, customers, and other stakeholders. It is amazing what you can learn about your operation's successes and pending failures when you let others, who are sometimes closer to the problem, tell you what they think.

Listening, real listening, isn't easy. It's more than just hearing. Not surprisingly, most people believe they are good listeners, yet we all know people do not absorb much of what they hear. Perhaps the most difficult component in effective listening is the ability to focus without being distracted by other ideas or tasks.

Secondly, you have to listen to more than words. When talking about sensitive issues, people often broach subjects obliquely. Listen for emotional content and incorporate your observations of the speaker's body language into your understanding of what is being said. To reduce the frequent misunderstandings we all find ourselves caught up in, paraphrase what you have heard and seek confirmation.

It is the province of knowledge to speak, and it is the privilege of wisdom to listen.
—Oliver Wendell Holmes

There are three basic styles of listening—competitive, attentive, and active. Competitive listening says that you are more interested in your own point of view than understanding someone else's viewpoint. You can read the presence of this listening style in people's body language: they appear ready to pounce. They may be quiet while someone else is talking, but it is obvious they can hardly wait to talk again. Their response suggests they didn't really hear anything much less think about what was said.

Dogs listen to you. Cats take a message and may get back to you later.
—Anonymous

Attentive listening shows genuine interest in understanding the other person's point of view, but there is no feedback to make it clear the message was correctly received.

Lastly is active or active listening. The person who practices active listening is interested in understanding what the other person is thinking, feeling, and wanting and in understanding what the message means. The active listener confirms their understanding of what the other person said before stating their own thoughts. The active listener will often restate or paraphrase the other's message for verification.

One thing a good listener does not do is interrupt. Perhaps this has happened to you—you're trying to find the right words, and bang, they finish your sentence. They are not listening; they are talking. This behavior immediately shuts down your employee or co-worker. This is a two-fold problem: First, you have just conveyed a negative message that may make future conversation less open. Second, you might miss some valuable information.

There are many opportunities to listen effectively during your routine activities. You can hear a lot of good ideas and information by walking into the building through the employee parking lot or in the elevator. You can also take advantage of listening opportunities in the cafeteria and by the coffee machine. When you are listening to someone, let them know. Give feedback. Tell them what you heard or understand and ask for clarification, if necessary.

Tips for Effective Listening

- You cannot listen and do something else at the same time.
- Establish eye contact, lean forward, have an open body posture and an accepting attitude that may include saying "uh-huh" or "go on" or nodding your head.
- Don't interrupt or finish someone else's sentences.
- Paraphrase what you have heard and check to make sure you "got it."
- Ask probing or clarifying questions.
- If action is requested or required, commit to it, and provide a time table for follow-up.

A case in point: In the fall of 1988, Jack Welch, the then chairman and CEO of General Electric, created a company-wide program called "Work-Out." Work-Out was aimed at capturing good ideas from employees and solving production problems. The Work-Out meeting was town-hall style with managers sitting on a stage and listening as employees told them what was wrong with their organization and how to fix it. Work-Out required the manager to respond to employee suggestions on the spot or, if more data were needed, no later than a couple days after the meeting. The speed of the required response and the method of delivering the observations required managers to have very effective listening skills and good follow-up questions. The Work-Out meetings were a success at GE because Welch trusted his first-line supervisors to properly execute the Work-Out effort. Variations of this have been adopted in countless other companies as a change-management and problem-solving tool. It's a great mechanism to discover what's going on in your employees' heads.[xiv]

Br

Brainstorming

Brainstorming is a group activity to stimulate creative thinking. During brainstorming, a group produces as many ideas related to a topic as possible, without criticism or judgment. Brainstorming can be a productive and enlivening process, or it can be a complete waste of everyone's time — it's all in the execution.

The concept of brainstorming is credited to Alex Osborn from writings in the early 1940s. Brainstorming uses ideas from a group of people to solve a challenge such as marketing a new product, decreasing errors in production, or fund raising. It can be any vexing issue your current methods are not solving. A brainstorming meeting may include employees from different backgrounds or perspectives on the problem.

In a brainstorming session, attendees may call out ideas, or you can go around the room and give each person their chance to offer a suggestion. The ideas generated should be accepted without criticism or praise, and someone must be tasked with writing down the ideas for future consideration. After a list is generated, the group discusses the ideas, refining or combining some. The goal of brainstorming is the quantity of ideas, not quality. Evaluation of quality and workability is accomplished later.

One key concept to effectively use the brainstorming tool is to precisely identify the challenge. A poorly conceptualized topic can lead the group in unproductive directions or fail to lead the group toward useful solutions. Many experts believe that the senior or project manager should not be present at brainstorming sessions because their presence may inhibit creative or even outrageous ideas. Often brainstorming sessions are employee-led, but some organizations use trained facilitators to manage the logistics of the meeting and ensure compliance with general brainstorming rules.

Guidelines for Effective Brainstorming

- Include a diverse group of employees in the meeting; six to twelve is about the right number of attendees.
- Clearly and precisely state the problem to be solved — be sure everyone understands the problem before generating ideas.
- Accept all ideas without judgment or criticism.

- Generate as many ideas as possible—do not worry about feasibility.
- Write down the ideas generated using a whiteboard or flipchart.
- Do not discuss an idea during the session—just capture it on the list.
- Make no decisions.

71

Re

Take responsibility

Taking responsibility is tough; it requires acting at the most excruciating time. Responsibility is accepting that only you have control over your thoughts, actions, and feelings—it means accepting accountability for the consequences of your actions.

In a poignant example, National Security Council Terrorism Advisor Richard A. Clark apologized after the 9/11 attacks, saying, "Your government failed you. Those entrusted with protecting you failed you. And I failed you." He later faced the 9/11 families during commission testimony and said, "We tried hard. But that doesn't matter because we failed. And for that failure, I would ask, once all the facts are out, for your understanding and for your forgiveness."[xv]

Taking responsibility requires timely action instead of waiting until you are forced to by circumstances. Managers want employees to take responsibility just as parents want children to be responsible. In organizations, responsibility is a crucial value that has to be modeled by its leadership.

Responsible people are dependable; they do what needs to be done, they don't make excuses for their mistakes, and they exercise self- control. Reagan took full responsibility for the 1983 marine barracks bombing in Lebanon, and in 1980, Carter squarely shouldered responsibility for the failed Iranian hostage rescue attempt.

X

Suppress own ideas—execute theirs

Of course you have good ideas. You know a great deal about your operating environment, your stakeholders, and your obligations. However, your employees know parts of the operational picture you don't, and they probably know their jobs better than you do. Working collectively, teams are usually more creative than any one individual at coming up with possible solutions to business challenges.

When *you* attend a meeting and provide *your* ideas, most of your employees will stop thinking and start reacting. After all, you are in charge and have spoken. If this isn't the outcome you want, suppress many of your own ideas and facilitate discussions to generate employees' ideas. Best of all, when groups reach a consensus and own the ideas, they naturally buy into them and execute them more effectively than if the orders come from management. Your job is to provide guidance on expectations and any necessary boundaries, and then let the team work on solutions within those requirements.

A few ways to encourage staff to take part in problem solving or brainstorming sessions are:

- If you choose to attend the meeting, don't sit in the "lead" chair. It may even be beneficial to sit in different places during each meeting.
- Put someone else in charge of the meeting and rotate that responsibility.
- If the meeting stalls, ask a question—remember element 13, Ask "why" five times.
- As the group narrows the discussion to a couple of ideas or solutions, suggest they take those and focus on implementation tasks and timelines.
- After the group has settled on one or two approaches and is moving into tasking, ask what you can do to help make the plan succeed.

EXERCISES

Exercise 1
Practice Listening

One-on-one, spend five minutes discussing each of these four controversial topics.*

After each discussion, summarize what you heard and ask for feedback on your summary and your listening behaviors.

Controversial subjects offer more challenge in maintaining an open mind and a listening attitude than information-only topics.

Topics for Discussion

1. Who was the most effective U.S. president in the twentieth century?

2. Should the terms of Supreme Court justices be limited?

3. What impact do humans have on global warming?

4. Should marijuana be legalized for medical purposes?

Exercise 2
Brainstorming

You are in charge of a fund-raising event at your child's school. The principal has suggested a silent auction. Create a small group to brainstorm how to get donations for the auction.

List all the ideas the team comes up with. Make sure everyone has a chance to add ideas. What do you do next?

Brainstorming

1. _____
2. _____
3. _____
4. _____
5. _____
6. _____

Next: _____

EXERCISE 3: BEST AND WORST BOSSES

When you first began working for a living, you were probably not the manager or the leader; you were a trainee, a grunt, a gofer. Think back to that time then forward through your entire working career. What were the characteristics of your worst boss? Did he or she trust employees or just tell them what to do and stand over them to make sure they did it? What were characteristics of your best bosses in terms of how they treated employees? Use the table below to select the behavior characteristics of your best and worse managers using different colors of ink. See what behaviors you liked and respected and which behaviors you did not appreciate or find productive. Now, plot your own behaviors in terms of trusting others. How are you doing?

PLOT YOUR BEST & WORST BOSS

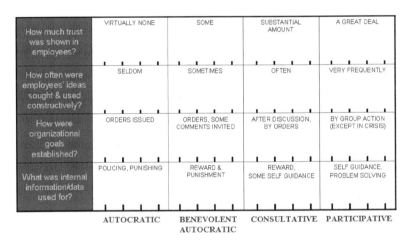

	VIRTUALLY NONE	SOME	SUBSTANTIAL AMOUNT	A GREAT DEAL
How much trust was shown in employees?				
How often were employees' ideas sought & used constructively?	SELDOM	SOMETIMES	OFTEN	VERY FREQUENTLY
How were organizational goals established?	ORDERS ISSUED	ORDERS, SOME COMMENTS INVITED	AFTER DISCUSSION, BY ORDERS	BY GROUP ACTION (EXCEPT IN CRISIS)
What was internal information/data used for?	POLICING, PUNISHING	REWARD & PUNISHMENT	REWARD, SOME SELF GUIDANCE	SELF GUIDANCE, PROBLEM SOLVING
	AUTOCRATIC	BENEVOLENT AUTOCRATIC	CONSULTATIVE	PARTICIPATIVE

Chapter 4: Get Feedback

It isn't possible to overestimate the importance of getting good feedback when leading and managing your organization. Feedback from your customers, employees, peers, and more senior managers provide a reality check that may confirm your observations or help you shift course quickly when circumstances change.

Feedback can be positive, negative, or neutral. Effective leaders are secure enough not to need their egos stroked. Rather, they understand that those around them have a vested interest in the organization and a perspective that is different from their own. They know that others can provide valuable insight into what needs to be done and the impact of what is planned or has been done.

It is your challenge and opportunity to seek out feedback through formal and informal means. You need to listen to the feedback, filter and process it, and then take action as necessary. You and the organization will both benefit from your efforts to get and use feedback.

What you will learn in this chapter:

Learning and communicating while wandering around
- What questions you should ask to better understand an employee's reality
- How to listen effectively

Making one-on-one meetings effective
- Using meeting time effectively
- Getting to know one another as people not positions

Using interactive off-sites
- How to set up a productive off-site meeting
- How to build teams

Getting useful information from surveys and polls
- Why you should use surveys and polls
- How to write survey questions that get the information needed to make decisions

Wa

Wander around

Executives at Hewlett-Packard developed the concept of "Management by Wandering Around" in the 1970s, and it became such a popular management technique that it was reduced to an acronym—MBWA. The problem was, it quickly became a fad, and some managers just wandered without listening and learning. The real goal of MBWA is not exercise but increasing interaction opportunities between senior management and employees. MBWA provides an informal opportunity to communicate your beliefs and values and improve the understanding of how implementation of your goals impacts direct-line employees.

Ask Questions:

How do you do that?

What happens next?

How long does it take?

Can we do this faster or better?

Can I help?

MBWA gives management firsthand knowledge of employee morale and the reality of life in the trenches. When a senior manager gets his travel voucher reimbursed in two days, he probably has no idea a lower-ranking engineer must wait forty-five days for his reimbursement to snake its way through accounting. When his presentations are typed by someone else and mailed that day, he may not know that salesmen wait three weeks for their presentations because of a backlog in the overworked media support group.

MBWA only works if you know how to use it—wandering, by itself, is not enough. It's critical to be skilled in the interaction component of MBWA. Ask questions like, "What are you doing?" (be sure to follow this question up with another question or you won't generally get a lot of information), "Could this task go better or faster if changes in the process were made?", "What would you recommend?", and most important, "How can I help?" Look for opportunities to comment on something about the employee as a person, and make a connection in a nonthreatening way.

In addition to walking through work and production areas, MBWA can be done in common areas like the parking lot, cafeteria, or a company exercise facility. At first, employees may suspect MBWA is just an excuse for managers to spy and interfere, but if you make MBWA a routine, it won't take long for it to become an accepted part of your company's culture and people will welcome your smiling visit. (Guidelines on how and when to use MBWA are suggested in the article by Chris Bell in Further Reading.)

Warning: There are courses on giving feedback but none on how to get it, yet the higher you climb in an organization, the less feedback (ground truth) you get from the bottom tier. MBWA is a good way to get feedback, so use it.

Humor Break

The importance of listening well—humor posted by Dr. Michelle Tempest on "The Psychiatrist's Blog" [xvi]

"As a psychiatrist I would say that possibly the most important, yet also the most under-rated of all skills is that of listening. The danger in not listening carefully to what is being said is illustrated by the following somewhat apocryphal transcript of which there are a number of different versions, this one being between a U.S. navy ship and a Canadian authority:

U.S. Navy: Please divert your course 15 degrees to the north to avoid a collision.
Canadians: Recommend you divert your course 15 degrees to the north to avoid a collision.
U.S. Navy: This is the captain of a U.S. Navy ship. I say again, divert your course.
Canadians: No. I say again, you divert your course.
U.S. Navy: This is the aircraft carrier USS Lincoln, the second largest ship in the United States' Atlantic fleet. We are accompanied by three destroyers, three cruisers and numerous support vessels. I demand that you change your course 15 degrees north, or counter-measures will be undertaken to ensure the safety of this ship.
Canadians: This is a lighthouse. Your call."

40

Oo

One-on-one meetings

Ensure focus—no calls or messages during meeting.

One-on-one meetings provide a unique opportunity to gauge attitudes and interests of your employees. A one-on-one meeting may be about good news shared privately, such as a promotion or a new project. Much less frequently, the meeting may involve disciplinary measures or bad news. In most cases, the private meeting may serve to get to know one another better and to build trust.

In formal meetings, practicing effective communication requires you to be concise, informative, realistic, and honest. You should give the person the information needed to do their jobs and to make decisions. Tell them not only what you think or what you want done but *why* you want it. Tell them what's in it for them and for the company.

An informal meeting has no obvious agenda and requires different communication skills. You need to consider the message you need to convey and the atmosphere you want to create. To be most effective, you need an environment that is comfortable and nonthreatening. You may select a neutral ground, like the cafeteria or a casual area in your office. One savvy CIA leader told me, "I never have anything between the other person and myself. Get out from behind that desk and have a more relaxed conversation." If you don't have a seating area in your office, consider moving your chair from behind the desk or arranging your desk against a wall so the chair faces out, removing obvious barriers between you and the other person.

The goal of the informal meeting is to share something of yourself and to learn about the employee—interests, likes, activities, etc. Practice good listening skills during the conversation. You can encourage discussion by showing an open, nonjudgmental body posture and making supportive comments that indicate you hear what is being said and understand. The business of your business may come up in the meeting, but it is not the purpose of it. Use this opportunity to find out what your employees think of their jobs, their perceptions of how they are treated and rewarded, or concerns they may have about getting their jobs done. You can also communicate through stories or examples from your experience to give the employee a sense of who you are behind the title.

In the end, you are still the boss, not a buddy. But you can use one–on–one meetings to build stronger relationships with your employees.

72

Io

**Interactive off-
sites**

There are many good reasons to hold an off-site meeting or activity. At an off-site, the interruptions are limited, especially if you have a rule about cell phones, messaging, and pagers. The goal of all off-site meetings is to encourage and facilitate interaction among employees. Different scenery often provokes creative problem solving and provides extra time together to build relationships that will remain in place long after the meeting is over. An off-site can be held down the street or may require air travel and overnight stays. Off-sites can be fun and educational.

An off-site meeting can be costly and needs to be well planned to be cost effective. You don't want your event to simply be a regular meeting at a different location. Whether you have an outside consultant or a designated staff member in charge of setting up and running the meeting, have someone in charge, not just someone to make the arrangements. In addition to planning, the coordinator should ensure that everyone understands the goals of the meeting and the expected outcome.

Hint: Never lead the off-site yourself. You can make opening and closing remarks, but then sit back, listen, and learn. The coordinator should be the one who takes care of follow-up for any ideas or action items that result from the off-site. In terms of planning, Bob Frisch, managing partner of Strategic Off-sites, says a useful metric is "four days of preparation for every day in the room."

Lonnie Pacelli provides guidance in "Team Building with a Purpose," as summarized in the following Making Your Off-site Work table. (A reference to the full text of his article can be found in Further Reading.)

Team Building with a Purpose

- Have a clear purpose and be sure everyone coming knows it.
- Have some fun scheduled in addition to meetings. Fun time may include dinners, snack breaks, nature walks, tours, or even ropes courses or challenge exercises.
- Facilitate networking through social time and meeting activities, especially if the participants work in different, physical locations.
- An overnight event provides unstructured time for team building and networking that is more difficult to accomplish during regular hours.
- Schedule the off-site to coincide with slower times at the office—if there are any—or move due dates to allow attendees to catch up. Discourage bringing work or computers to the meeting.
- Follow up with ideas and action items. This is important. Attendees need to see that some items were acted upon.

Honest feedback is an important component in making midcourse corrections to reach organizational goals. In this element, you are looking at internal surveys as opposed to customer satisfaction measures. For years, companies relied on employee surveys to collect feedback on management practices, company programs, and employee concerns. A multiple-choice questionnaire with perhaps a few open-ended questions was handed out, completed, and returned; then, the data was summarized and the results were passed up the management chain. In many cases, the results did not yield the actionable information hoped for due to a poorly structured questionnaire.

What do you need to know?

There are two, key components to getting useful information from survey data—good questions and honest answers. Let's look first at how to construct the survey questions. Ask yourself, "What do I want to know?" This is not the same as the list of questions on the survey. Rather, it is the information you need and the feedback that will impact your future behavior and decisions.

How will you extract and summarize the data?

Let's say you want feedback from employees about a new performance-based, bonus plan. If you ask questions like, "Do you like the new performance-based bonus?" you may get answers that reflect what you want to hear: "Yes sir, boss. You did well. We'll all work harder." But what you really want to know is whether the new, performance-based bonus will improve productivity and employee retention? You need to think harder about the components of the plan and ask questions that will provide clear feedback.

Who will use the data?

How will you report your findings?

In constructing a questionnaire, here are some other factors to keep in mind to improve the usability of responses:

What happens next?

- Your questionnaire should be one to four pages depending on the complexity and breadth of the issues being covered.
- Some organizations tack on too many interesting-to-know questions but never use the data. Resist this tendency. To avoid employee questionnaire fatigue, a few questions that generate actionable answers are far better than too many general questions.
- Ask general and specific questions in each area being surveyed.
- Multiple-choice and true/false questions are more likely to get a useful response than open-ended questions—use the former sparingly.
- Make sure a multiple-choice question accommodates all possible answers.
- Likert scale questions can be useful, but there is a tendency for

people to rarely mark extreme values, even if they hold them.

- Don't ask compound questions (e.g., Do you like the performance-based bonus and the new vacation plan?).
- Don't ask leading questions.
- Don't ask general, demographic questions unless you need to understand differences in perceptions across groups.

Here are a couple of additional considerations for survey questions: First, consider getting outside help in constructing your survey questions. There are solid research firms that specialize in this and may offer you constructive suggestions. A bonus to using a third-party survey is you can compare your results with other organizations. Second, run some test subjects through the questionnaire to assess validity and reliability. When you see the test run results, you may decide to tweak the questions.

After you have constructed and tested your survey, you have several options for collecting the answers. One is to use an online tool, like Survey Monkey, that allows the respondents to complete the questionnaire in privacy and anonymity. In general, an online questionnaire tends to provide the most cost effective option if the majority of your employees have Internet access. Whatever way you choose to collect data, the most important part of collecting and analyzing surveys is to share the results (many managers forget this). If actions are planned in response to the analysis of employee opinions, share that also.

General Employee Survey Areas

- Overall employee satisfaction with the organization and their job
- Specific employee views about
  - Leadership
  - Planning
  - Vision
  - Corporate culture
  - Work environment
- Communication
  - Clarity
  - Frequency
  - Coverage
  - Usefulness
- Benefits (ask about each separately)
- Training availability and utility
- Effectiveness and responsiveness of immediate supervisors and the chain of command

EXERCISES

Exercise 1
Management by Walking
Around

What should you do?

You are practicing MBWA. For each of these situations, what do you do next?

1. An employee comes up and begins complaining about his current assignment.

2. A group of employees are gathered around the coffeepot discussing a new product your company is offering.

3. There is a rumor going around that the organization will be laying-off workers next quarter. This is a possible but unlikely action.

Exercise 2
Survey and Poll

Constructing a survey and poll on change in benefits package

You have just changed carriers for your organization's health insurance. The new policy is more costly for the individual employee, but also offers more choices to tailor coverage to individual and family needs.

How can you use "Survey and Poll" to understand the impact of the change?

1. List five questions you want answered about the new carrier and health care benefits (these are not survey questions but what management needs to know to make future decisions).

2. What questions would you ask your employees?

3. Should you collect demographic information from the respondents? If so, why? If not, why not?

4. If the majority of your employees really dislike the new plan, what action would you take to communicate the survey results?

Chapter 5: Lead People

Why is Martin Luther King's "I Have a Dream" speech considered one of the one hundred best speeches in American history? Because King provided his audience with a vision of the future and a clear set of expectations for what fulfilling the dream would mean to members of the audience, and he spoke with a passion that moved the audience and changed behaviors.

As a leader, you must articulate a vision of your organization's future and then motivate others to share it—you can't be their leader if you don't know where you are taking them. You don't have to be as eloquent as Dr. King but note how his dream wasn't too specific—it left room in the minds of his followers to fill in the details. Had Moses gone into too much detail about property boundaries, local governance, and water rights, he could never have led the Jews to escape from Egypt to the promised land.

Like Teddy Roosevelt leading the charge on horseback and foot in the battle for San Juan Hill, you need to translate and communicate what you deeply believe in order to enlist the hearts of your employees and instill them with a shared vision and commitment—that's the first step in changing behaviors.

You demonstrate through your own behavior that you believe in the vision, and you assist them in aligning their behavior and beliefs to reach the same destination. You don't have to be Hannibal leading his troops over the Alps—this works for average people too.

Software salesman Todd Beamer called out, "Let's roll" to lead his fellow passengers on flight 93 in the first counter-attack on terrorism after the Pentagon and Twin Towers strike. In a 1999 Little Rock, Arkansas, runway incident, flight 1420 passengers were led to safety shortly before the plane exploded by members of a college choir.

Employees want to be inspired, and they appreciate being part of a larger purpose. In this chapter, we look at vision, expectations, and even passion to see how you can translate your vision into action.

What you will learn in this chapter:

What is an organizational vision
- Why having a vision is important
- Examples of visions and visionaries

How your expectations drive employee performance
- Modeling expected values
- Communicating expectations

Showing the relationship between the desired future and today's behaviors
- The role of leadership in having and showing direction
- Components of effective direction

Passionate leaders beget passionate employees
- The importance of passion in your work
- Communicating your passion to motivate and educate

23

Vi

Vision

Jeff Bezos had a vision that the Internet would completely change brick-and-mortar-based retailing. Bill Gates believed that individuals would want to own personal computers. Muhammad Yunus believed that small amounts of money, carefully placed in developing countries, could change the world. These leaders had vision. So what is vision, and why should you care?

Vision without action is a daydream. Action without vision is a nightmare.
—*Japanese proverb*

Good business leaders create a vision, articulate the vision, passionately own the vision, and relentlessly drive it to completion.
—*Jack Welch*

Your vision is where you want your organization to be in the future—not next year, but in the next three to five years. Vision represents your beliefs about what will happen and what matters. Your vision drives your decision making and inspires your employees to move in a common direction. As opposed to your mission statement, your company's vision is internal. It is the glass through which you view the future and make decisions today. Your "vision statement" gives employees a sense of purpose, helping them see themselves as "building a cathedral rather than laying stones." (Further reading: Small Business Notes)[xvii]

When he launched the national newspaper *USA Today* twenty-five ago, Allen Neuharth, CEO of Gannett Company from 1973–86, was derided by both Wall Street analysts and the newspaper establishment: "Who would want to buy news snippets instead of real stories?" they asked. The answer was millions of people would, eventually making *USA Today* the leading newspaper in the country. Neuharth had a vision of what could be, and more importantly, he had the ability to communicate that vision to his employees and stakeholders.[xviii]

Working without a business vision leaves your organization susceptible to distraction at the hands of quarterly performance profiles or daily firefighting. Having a vision is like having a rudder—it lets you steer a course toward your goals. You do not need vision to have a successful organization, but if you want to grow, change, and leave something behind when you are gone, then having vision is a must.

41

Se

Set expectations

Setting expectations is a key responsibility of leaders and managers in all organizations. This responsibility includes setting the expectations for the organization as a whole, for departments within the organization, and for individuals within departments. Expectations must be clearly stated and shared using both written and oral communication.

Some expectations are measurable and time delimited, such as "complete product redesign by June 30." These are job or task expectations. Other expectations, those that are closely tied to organizational values, are more conceptual, such as Starbucks's Five-Ways-of-Being (Be welcoming, Be genuine, Be considerate, Be knowledgeable, Be involved), which tell employees how to work with customers, each other, and management.

The intent of element 41—Set expectations—is more like the Starbucks example. These expectations are part of inspiring and leading. As a leader, you provide guidance on how to implement core values to reach strategic goals. Critical to getting your expectations met is modeling the behaviors you expect your employees to exemplify. Next, set expectations through formal and informal communication using lists, handouts, stories, and vignettes that show employees how your expectations play out in the real world. Finally, reward those who meet expectations, and correct those who do not.

Here are some strategies to successfully accomplish these two tasks:

Guidelines for Setting and Communicating Expectations

- Guidelines for Setting and Communicating Expectations
- Set realistic expectations based on judgment and data.
- Tell people what you're doing, what you expect to happen, and when you expect it to happen.
- For more conceptual expectations, explain with stories and vignettes, not just words.
- Consider and explain how you will measure compliance with expectations.
- Tell people what you expect of them as workers and as corporate citizens.
- Consider and explain how expectations build to strategic accomplishments.
- Ask questions to make sure employees understand expectations.

73

Di

Have/show direction

Having and showing direction is like providing a roadmap to a destination. As a leader and manager, your task is to establish the desired goal (the destination) and the objectives that must be accomplished along a timeline to reach that state. You identify the direction the organization needs to follow based on data, insight, and analysis. Your direction moves the organization where it needs to be to remain viable and successful. Delegate the tactics employed to those more closely associated with task execution to reach your objectives. Your roadmap of goals and objectives must be clearly articulated and provide context that allows your employees to move independently toward your mutually agreed upon destination.

A key component of having and showing direction involves establishing performance boundaries in terms of time, cost, and risk management. It's your job to generate excitement to motivate those executing the roadmap. You accomplish this through
- Leading by example
- Providing feedback
- Removing barriers,
- Mentoring
- Empowering your staff.

The Process Improvement Roadmap illustrates short-term direction requiring measurable process improvement and a schedule to reach the goal, responsibilities, costs, and outcome measures.

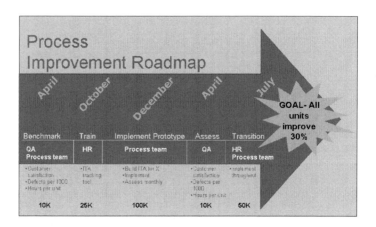

Process Improvement Roadmap

April | October | December | April | July

GOAL- All units improve 30%

Benchmark	Train	Implement Prototype	Assess	Transition
QA Process team	HR	Process team	QA	HR Process team
•Customer satisfaction •Defects per 1000 •Hours per unit	•ITA tracking tool	•Build ITA for X •Implement •Assess monthly	•Customer satisfaction •Defects per 1000 •Hours per unit	•Implement throughout
10K	25K	100K	10K	60K

Risk more than others think safe.

Dream more than others think practical.

Expect more than others think possible.

Care more than others think wise.
—Howard Schultz
Founder of Starbucks
Coffee

We reserve the word passion to describe those activities or products that we really believe in and want to share with others. When you are passionate about an activity, you do it for the sheer pleasure it gives you, and you want it (whatever it is) to be the best. You want to make a difference in something larger than your life—you want to change the lives of others.

To be more effective, you must share your passion any time you enlist others in your quest. You want your employees to help you realize the corporate mission.

People want to be inspired. They want to be part of something meaningful and successful. According to Richard Chang, author of *The Passion Plan at Work: Building a Passion-Driven Organization,* "Passion is the single most powerful competitive advantage an organization can claim in building its success." Stressing that passion is a motivator and a unifier, that it provides direction and focus, and attracts both employees and customers, Chang suggests that when a company has the skills and resources it needs to succeed, "passion can put it over the top." Chang cites passionate organizations such as MindSpring, Southwest Airlines, and Ben & Jerry's as examples that demonstrate what passion is and how it supports accomplishing corporate missions and achieving profitability.

If you are passionate about your organization, a product, or an idea, how do you communicate that passion? Here are some suggestions:

- Explain your vision of how the future can be – with and without your product, idea or service
- Use examples and provocative phrases (look at the speeches of Martin Luther King or Winston Churchill for excellent examples of passion-based inspiration)
- Show your excitement and commitment through your own work-life
- Incorporate the ideas of others than facilitate reaching your vision
- Help your employees feel part of something important, something transformative – tell them about the difference they are making
- Work hard at translating your passion into examples and actions that your employees can relate to

EXERCISES

Exercise 1

Communicating Your Vision

What do you say about:

An acquaintance who teaches an introductory business class at a local university has asked you to sit on a discussion panel about what is required to successfully operate a business. You hope to find some promising interns for your company in this class.

1. Your organization today and how you became successful

2. What it means to work at your company

3. Your vision for the future

Exercise 2

Leading People

Characteristics of a Leader

You learn to be a better leader by emulating the behavior of leaders you respect as well as developing your own natural leadership style. Think about men or women who have been in leadership positions over you, and answer these questions.

1. What were the characteristics of leaders that motivated you to follow them?

2. Did others respond in the same way? If not, why do you think they were not persuaded?

3. Can you think of ways that these leaders could have been more effective?

Chapter 6: Motivate

Unless you work entirely by yourself, your organization gets where you want it to be by the labor and commitment of others. Your chances for success improve by providing a vision, acting as a role model, and having a set of corporate values that others are proud to be part of.

Motivating is more than cheerleading. You can motivate your team and your organization by helping them become part of the solution, making expectations of results crystal clear, and delegating responsibility and decision-making authority. You boost motivation further by removing performance barriers so employees can accomplish their tasks more easily.

It is your job to help your staff see how their collective behavior affects the organization. Motivate your employees by continually rewarding desired performance monetarily and, more importantly, with recognition. People want to be part of a successful enterprise, and sharing your vision, knowledge, values, and enthusiasm can help them achieve their goals and yours.

The business value of delegation and empowerment
- What is the difference
- What is the impact on your organization

Why you must be an enabler
- What are performance barriers
- What you can do to remove barriers

Leadership requires accountability
- To whom are you accountable
- What does being accountable mean

The business value of sharing information
- Ways to formally share information
- Ways to create an information sharing environment

When done correctly, delegation can be one of a boss's greatest gifts to employees. Delegation is not simply unloading work on others; it's giving them authority to act. When you delegate a task or an objective to someone else, you are asking that person to be responsible, to take charge, to get it done. You send a strong message that you trust them to complete the task.

Note: Empowering someone is subtly different from delegating to them. To empower someone implies that you also provide them with skills, information, authority, and resources to carry out their responsibilities. Delegation and empowerment show your employees that you trust them to use their knowledge and judgment in a way that is consonant with your values to reach your goals. You delegate and empower others so more work can be accomplished and so you can spend your time on tasks where you add the most value.

Delegation and empowerment have a side benefit—employees feel more a part of the team. To effectively delegate or empower someone to accomplish a task or reach a goal, make sure that person fully understands the expected outcome. Most organizations miss the crucial step of educating employees on desired outcomes and how they are linked to the overall mission.

Initially, you may spend more time effectively delegating than doing the task yourself, but remember, doing everything yourself in the long run is a very inefficient and unmotivating strategy for your employees.

Evolution of Empowerment

Total Decision Control	Accept Input	Share Power	Distribute Power
Impose decisions	Consult with employees	Make Decisions jointly	Employees have authority to make decisions

One of the most important services you provide for organizational health and well-being is to remove the barriers that impede your employee's ability to do their jobs. Barriers may be the unintended consequences of business processes or inefficient ways of doing business. These barriers cost time, energy, and money and frustrate your employees.

Enabling is the flip side of the coin—it is a proactive approach to getting things done by making tools and processes available and, most importantly, by providing training and authority.

The *American Heritage Dictionary* defines an enabler as someone who supplies the means, knowledge, or opportunity—this is what you want to be. Empower employees to make changes when it helps get the task done faster, better, or cheaper. For example, if an employee believes that customer service can be more responsive and timely by changing a data-collection form, assure them that they have permission and provide resources to try the change on a small sample. If it works, then use it. If not, you have still shown your employees that you will help them help the organization—you were an enabler.

How can you remove barriers and become an enabler? Here are some successful strategies:

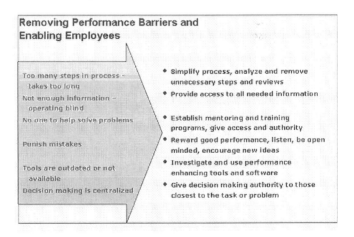

Removing Performance Barriers and Enabling Employees

Too many steps in process – takes too long	• Simplify process, analyze and remove unnecessary steps and reviews
Not enough information – operating blind	• Provide access to all needed information
No one to help solve problems	• Establish mentoring and training programs, give access and authority
Punish mistakes	• Reward good performance, listen, be open minded, encourage new ideas
Tools are outdated or not available	• Investigate and use performance enhancing tools and software
Decision making is centralized	• Give decision making authority to those closest to the task or problem

Ac

Accountability

This is a very powerful element. Accountability means to account for your actions. In business, accountability is sometimes used synonymously with responsibility. However, there is a distinction: you can delegate responsibility to a subordinate to accomplish a task, but you can't delegate your accountability for the outcome.

The definition of accountability is changing as we learn more about employee performance. Under the old definition, accountability meant being subjected to blame. The new definition involves making sure everyone understands and lives up to expected outcomes. That isn't easy to attain because we know from Gallup polling that most employees do not fully understand what is expected of them at work, which is the first part of the new definition.

One of the strongest chemical reactions on our Periodic Table occurs when you mix lots of this element with lots of empowerment to produce high performance. When you do, employees are linked to your mission — they know how they fit in and what is expected (accountability). For your part, get out of the way, give them resources, and let them accomplish (empowerment).

Accountability means

Resources	Employees	Results
-Planning	-Share information	-Delegate
-Asset management	-Treat everyone fairly	-Deliver
-Align spending to revenues	-Acknowledge failures	-Measure
-Use staff wisely	-Recognize achievements	-Communicate

Everyone understands, appreciates, and lives up to expected outcomes

We've all heard the saying "give a man a fish, and he will eat for a day. Teach a man to fish, and he will eat for a lifetime." Think of your employees as knowledge fishermen. They collect data and information and convert it to actionable knowledge. That knowledge, accumulated over decades of work, is a valuable asset. It becomes even more valuable when it's shared. If knowledge sharing is not integral in your organization, everyone has to learn from scratch every time.

If you have knowledge, let others light their candles in it.[xix]
—Margaret Fuller

Most organizations have formal processes for sharing knowledge through classes, mentoring, peer group discussion, formal apprenticeship, corporate libraries, and data bases. There are also informal processes that spring up in a supportive environment, such as chats, walking-around management, focus groups, and red teams. Finding effective ways to share corporate knowledge is so important that entire college courses are devoted to knowledge sharing techniques, and consulting firms have sprouted along with a professional discipline, with associated software tools, for knowledge management.

Element 106 (Share knowledge and resources) is about attitude. It's your attitude and the corporate cultural that encourage everyone to offer their knowledge and ideas about accomplishing an objective, solving a problem, or using resources.

Case study from the CIA: Kelly, a first-rate support employee, herded all her co-workers into a room, separated them into two teams, and challenged each team to come up with as many ideas for improving the work environment or work processes as possible. After an hour, the team that came up with the most ideas would win the competition, but here's where it got interesting.

Kelly knew that without proper execution, ideas can be rather cheap. After the teams returned from their brainstorming, she declared an idea didn't count unless someone on the other team agreed to take ownership and implement it. "You get one point for each idea you generated and two points for each idea you sell the other group to implement." Several hours of haggling ensued as the groups tried to sell ideas to one another. If swapping failed or a group couldn't convince the other to adopt an idea, a member within the originating group could take ownership and implement the idea for one point.

With much laughter and lots of collaboration, over forty great improvement ideas were implemented within two weeks, improving work life and mission performance.

EXERCISES

Exercise 1
Knowledge Sharing

Your organization has just won a large development contract, and you will be increasing your staff by 25 percent. Think of five actions you can take to capture and share knowledge about the project and previous effective project management techniques with your new team.

Methods to Share Knowledge

1. _____

2. _____

3. _____

4. _____

5. _____

Exercise 2
Practicing Accountability

Being accountable means owning your behavior and its consequences. Pick two examples from your experience or observation – one positive example of someone stepping up to their responsibilities and one negative. For each example, list the long-term effects of the person's actions.

Long-term Effects of Acting with Accountability

1. _____
   _____
   _____

2. _____
   _____
   _____

Chapter 7: Engage the Workforce

No one wants to work on a task in a threatening or unpleasant environment. Common sense tells us that, but surveys and studies completed over the last five years now firmly link employee performance to how people are treated in a work environment. People want to enjoy their work and the camaraderie of peers. People also work better when they are part of a team working toward a common objective. They want to be trusted, respected, and engaged in the outcome.

When the team is pulling in the same direction and believes in the same mission, the benefits to the organization are immeasurable. People look forward to coming to work, they add their creativity to solving problems, and they willingly take responsibility to improve the value for all stakeholders.

As a leader and manager, you set the tone of the workplace. Therefore, you have it within your power to get the workforce engaged in caring about meeting objectives and outcomes. It is a huge part of your job to get employees enthusiastically involved in the process. Create a feeling of shared purpose and trust, and you need to allow and encourage everyone to have fun along the way.

The importance of play
- Why incorporating play with work improves productivity
- Some ways to add fun to routine tasks

The importance of admitting mistakes
- When should you admit a mistake and to whom
- What can you learn from mistakes

Leaders are approachable people
- The value to you and the organization of being approachable
- How to demonstrate approachability

The value of reciprocity
- What is reciprocity in an organizational environment
- Types of corporate reciprocity

People rarely succeed unless they have fun in what they are doing.[xx]
—*Dale Carnegie*

Fun is good.[xxi]
—*Dr. Seuss*

We sometimes think of play as being the opposite of work. Mark Twain said, "Work and play are words used to describe the same thing under differing conditions." We may think play is fun and work is well, work. But if you think of play as a way of feeling, then play can happen at any time.

Play can be described as a light-hearted, recreational activity. When you play, it is okay to be imaginative, laugh, and be a bit silly. When you are playing, you are free, relaxed, happy, and having fun. IDEO corporation successfully uses play to attain remarkable innovation. The reason for their success is based on sound science—play affects the cerebral cortex, where thinking takes place.

When you think about how people feel when they are playing, then you can imagine that there are times when play at work is a good thing. Play at work helps relieve tension, makes interactions more enjoyable, and builds bonds of joint purposefulness.

Play is an attitude—a quality of the mind. Seek opportunities to feel like you are playing. If you approach a task with an "oh no, not again" attitude, that's what you will experience. (For an interesting look at play, go the National Institute for Play Web site at www.nifplay.org.)

When you were younger, do you remember an experience when playfulness made an unpleasant task more enjoyable? For example, when you had cleanup duty for an event and the cleanup crew sang songs while they worked, wasn't the task more fun and didn't the task get done more quickly? Or when you were taking a long car ride and you played games with your siblings or parents, it made the time go faster.

Play improves learning and socialization. As a leader and manager, there are many opportunities in the execution of daily tasks that can be improved with a touch of play. Below are some examples of ways you can inject play into otherwise non-fun activities:

NOT FUN	PLAYFUL and FUN
All-day meetings	• Start with ten minutes to socialize. • Have some interactive tasks—vary the format. • Use humor in presentations (element 1), and don't forget a good cartoon within all those Power Point slides. • Have live demonstrations or field trips. • Be irreverent at times.
Deadlines—long hours	• Have an ice cream social on Friday afternoon. • Equip a snack area with fresh fruit and some toys or games. • Organize sports or game nights to work off some stress.
Drab surroundings	• Have a showcase for employees' favorite pet pictures, favorite cartoons, funny photos, or children's' art. • Encourage employees to decorate their spaces, and give them the freedom to add some fun. • Sponsor a "bring your pet to work day."
Same stuff, different day	• When appropriate to their job, give employees some time each week to work on a fun personal project—this has been done successfully at Google and resulted in some profitable products. • Replace some standard office supplies—like sticky notes—with some that are humorous. • Build a humor board in a common area for jokes, cartoons, or funnies.
Travel	• Learn something about each city you visit, and schedule a chance to see a unique feature. • Keep a library of books and articles to read on airplanes and airports.

Am

Admit mistakes

Mistakes are about actions, not outcomes. People make mistakes. Avoid making the same mistake again; admit the one you made, and learn from the experience. As a leader, your mistakes may affect more people than your employees' mistakes, so it is important that you learn quickly and move on. Admitting a mistake is the first step in taking responsibility and avoiding the same mistake in the future. Failure to admit a mistake leads to denials of the obvious, compounding mistakes, and a loss of credibility.

To whom do you admit a mistake? It depends. You may admit a mistake to your project team, your management, or your shareholders. The process of admitting the mistake should include lessons learned and plans to rectify. In order to understand your mistake and therefore learn from it, Scott Berkun, author of *The Art of Project Management* and teacher of critical thinking at the University of Washington, suggests that you work backward[xxii] incrementally from the end state beginning with moments then hours and finally days before the actual event to understand the contributing factors. (A link to his entire article can be found in Further Reading.)

Once you admit a mistake was made and understand the context, you and your colleagues can learn to avoid that mistake in the future. Here are some questions Berkun suggests you ask to help understand a mistake and learn from it:

- What was the probable sequence of events?
- Were there multiple, small mistakes that led to a larger one?
- Were there any erroneous assumptions made?
- Did we have the right goals?
- Were we trying to solve the right problem?
- Was it possible to have recognized bad assumptions earlier?
- Was there information we know now that would have been useful then?
- What would we do differently in this exact situation again?
- How can we avoid getting into situations like this?
- Was this simply unavoidable given all of the circumstances? A failure isn't a mistake if you were attempting the impossible.
- Has enough time passed for us to know if this was a mistake or not?

Be

Be approachable

Step one: *when they walk in—get your fingers off that keyboard!*

Your body language and your behavior tell someone more clearly than your words whether it is all right or even desirable to approach you. You learned to read body language when you were barely out of diapers. When your mom was standing in the kitchen, arms akimbo, scowling at the dog who had just tracked mud across the clean, kitchen floor, you knew it wasn't a good time to approach her and ask for a cookie.

Every boss says he or she has an "open-door policy," but that isn't enough. You want to be approachable to engage your staff, to hear what they have to say, to solicit their feedback, and to share your insights, instructions, and feedback. So how do you ensure your behavior and body language are consonant with your goal of being approachable?

Warning: You only have to send out one or two negative approach signals to ensure employees never approach you again.

First, if you know that you do not have time to engage in conversation, close your door. If you do not have a door, signal your lack of availability by being busy and not establishing eye contact when someone approaches. If you are available and want to be approached, do the opposite—establish eye contact, smile encouragingly, and ask a question or make a welcoming statement. Here are some guidelines for communicating to your staff that you are approachable:

Demonstrating that You Are Approachable

- Smile, establish eye contact, ask the employee(s) to sit with you.
- Listen to them, nod your head, give feedback, and ask questions.
- Sit comfortably with your arms open rather than folder across your body and lean forward.
- Allow a few minutes for chitchat before you dive into work topics.
- Attend exclusively to those with whom you are talking—do not take calls, read e-mail, or look through papers on your desk.
- If you are practicing "wandering around" (element 22), smile, establish eye contact, ask questions, and wait for a response.
- Maintain a relaxed, open, body position.
- Address staff by name.
- Give examples from your own experience.
- Use humor (element 1).

- Remove physical roadblocks, such as your desk, and stand or sit close enough for intimacy but not too close for cultural comfort.
- Say thank you.

107

Tr

Think reciprocity

In cultural anthropology, "reciprocity" defines the informal exchange of goods and labor. Reciprocity is also the basis of principles likes The Golden Rule, and we'll see in a moment why reciprocity is one of the most important elements. In social and business interactions, reciprocity can occur in three ways:

- **Generalized reciprocity** occurs when one person shares goods or labor with another person without expecting anything in return. This "giving" reciprocity is seen in parent–child interactions and improves trust and decreases social distance.
- **Balanced or symmetrical reciprocity** occurs when someone gives to someone else but expects a fair return in the future.
- **Bartering** is a reciprocal process with payment agreed beforehand – like swapping dollars for goods and labor.

Ever wonder why you get all those "gifts" of personalized address labels in the mail? The norm of reciprocity is at work – we feel compelled to try and repay what someone else has provided us. One study showed that mail survey requests that included a "gift" had a 65 percent higher response rate than those that didn't.

Politicians use the "norm of reciprocity" to influence others – just think about all those earmark gifts to constituents. President Lyndon Johnson mastered the art of favor giving to friends and opponents, which allowed him to pass large amounts of legislation.

A few people go beyond using reciprocity to influence and use it to manipulate. Peoples Temple leader, Jim Jones, showered his cult members with special favors. In 1978, one cult member, Diane Louie, was sick and refused special food from Jones because "I knew once he gave me those privileges, he'd have me. I didn't want to owe him nothing."[xxiii] Diane Louie escaped while over nine hundred cult members more directly under

Jones' control died following his orders to consume a cyanide-laced grape drink.

Stephen Covey, author of *The Seven Habits of Highly Effective People*, uses the phrase "emotional bank account" to describe the principle of reciprocity in relationships. The emotional bank account describes the trust that accumulates in a relationship. Of course, you need to make deposits before you make withdrawals, so before you think about getting, take the first step to give.

Practice reciprocity to build trust between management, employees, and key stakeholders. To serve as a role model, be the first to engage in reciprocal behaviors. What can you give on your side of the exchange? Try elements 21, 98, 95, or 24 (Listen, Valuing their opinions, Show concern, or Delegate).

Important Note: Review the Periodic Table. See the small green line under each of the eighteen columns labeled "Inspires Trust"? Reciprocity is an act, and trust is a by-product of reciprocity. Almost every one of the 118 elements is a good first step for you to build trust.

EXERCISES

Exercise 1
Learning to Play

Your team will be writing a magazine for distribution to staff and customers. Have them brainstorm what would be placed in the Table of Contents, the cover image, and the feature story.

Magazine Cover Mock-up

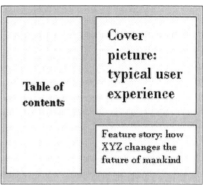

Table of contents

Cover picture: typical user experience

Feature story: how XYZ changes the future of mankind

Exercise 2
Approachability

The next time you are at a social event where people are expected to mingle and chat, be an observer for awhile. Note who is approached and think about their body language or verbalizations. Also find someone who seems off by themselves. Note their body language and verbalizations. How are they different? Can you tell why one was approached and the other was not?

Long-term Effects of Acting with Accountability

Describe the behavior of the person who was approached frequently:

_____

_____

_____

Describe the behavior of the person who was not approached:

_____

_____

Chapter 8: Give Feedback

Introduction:

Giving feedback is more than important—it is essential. Meaningful and useful feedback is the only guaranteed way to improve performance. As a manager and leader, you have a unique view of the organization, the outside world, and the interaction between the two. From your position you know what needs to be done and what effect an employee's current behaviors are having on the organization.

Use feedback to increase the frequency of desired behaviors and decrease the frequency of undesired behaviors, but always emphasize the positive. A 2003 study by the Corporate Executive Board showed that if you emphasize the negative in feedback, you generate negative performance. Let me repeat that: if you emphasize the negative in feedback, you generate negative performance. Feedback may be verbal, written, or symbolic. When feedback is objective, well timed, sincere, and directly related to employee behaviors, it makes an extraordinary difference.

Likewise, the absence of feedback creates a vacuum that causes anxiety and stagnation. Employees want to know how well they are doing, and you need them to know when they are right on target and when they should modify their behaviors to better meet the organization's expectations. Giving feedback is one of your most powerful management tools.

Establishing processes to collect feedback data, such as outcome measures, is important for any organization. As leader and manager, require all plans and processes have associated feedback loops to help the organization know how it is doing and to know when it needs to change. Use the objective knowledge gleaned from outcome measures to provide feedback to your employees about themselves and the organization.

What you will learn in this chapter:

Saying thank you pays dividends
- The most effective way to say thank you
- Optional activities to convey thanks

The value of offering to help
- Why *you* should be a helper
- The difference between helping and teaching

Celebrating success breeds more success
- Your role in celebrating success

- Tailoring celebrations to achievements

Using outcome measures

- Why you have to have outcome measures
- Types of useful outcome measures

26

Th

Say thanks

Merci beaucoup

Danke schön

Shukriya

Toda raba

Domo arigato

Gracias

Saying thank you is more than just being polite. It recognizes at a personal level the contribution of an employee to the organization. It feels good to be thanked — to have your effort acknowledged. It also feels good to do the thanking because it makes a difference.

There are several things you should include in your thanks. First, make your thank you timely — as close to the event as possible. Second, make your thank you sincere. Bad bosses don't understand why someone should be thanked for "just doing their job." Third, include with your thank-you a brief explanation of why the person is being thanked (e.g., "Thanks Sam, you did a great job getting that shipment out on time given all the problems with the handler.").

Besides saying the words "thank you," what else can you do to say thanks? One of the most powerful and meaningful ways to say thanks is to pass along a compliment from someone else. If a customer or vendor tells you how much they enjoyed working with Sally or appreciated Tom's special attention — pass that compliment along. Sally will feel good about being thanked and doubly good because you know about it too. You can write a personal note saying "thank you." For really extraordinary performance in the face of significant challenges, it may be appropriate to thank employee(s) with a reward, such as a dinner or movie certificate or even a performance bonus.

Here is an example of making "thank you" meaningful. At a large defense contractor, the employees had been putting in a lot of overtime to get a job done — missing evenings and weekends with families. At the completion of the project, the company sent a thank you to their spouses and significant others with a complementary dinner certificate and a personal note saying how much the company appreciated the sacrifices the family had made to get the job done. That thoughtfulness and understanding improved morale and helped the next time the group met a scheduling challenge.

Offering help is different than taking over a task. Your experience lets you help in additional ways that can be quite valuable to employees. Offering to help someone else is an opportunity to share knowledge (element 106), to provide direct reinforcement and feedback, and most important, to model how you want your employees to collaborate and support the mission.

Offering help can go outside the workplace. After hiring Mike Phillips, Faith Roland, a supervisor at Overland, Pacific & Cutler in Kirkland, Washington, helped him find a place to live. She went an extra step by taking Phillips and his girlfriend to a Seattle Mariner's game and conspired with Phillips to place a marriage proposal on the large, digital screen. (Incidentally, the girlfriend said yes.)

A good metaphor for offering help is the player/coach—someone who was a great player helping less-experienced players. A great example of this is René, a Popeye's fast food manager from El Salvador. Rene has what is called in the fast-food industry an MBA—a Mop Bucket Attitude. The voice of experience, Rene rolls up his sleeves to work alongside the crew in cleaning, cashiering, and cooking. He's a model for the standards he wants and provides a great example of reciprocity (element 107). His high-profit store is neat-as-a-pin, yet you hear lots of laughter (element 1), and when a great player/coach like Rene tells you you did a good job, it has a credibility that a compliment from an outsider can't match.

You can be a player/coach for your organization. Just roll up your sleeves like Mike Kirk, assistant operations chief of the Vashon Island Fire and Rescue. He starts the day with a funny anecdote, and then helps wash the fire trucks. Like René, he has an MBA.

Using your expertise to help others lets you create a workforce that moves your organization over many hurdles faster, better, and cheaper.

Cs

Celebrate Success

℄ELEBRATE

You just won a new contract or met a key milestone. Great! It's time to celebrate. Celebrate success to acknowledge everyone's contribution in achieving the goal. Celebrate success because it feels good to take a breather and pat your collective selves on the back for a job well done. Celebrations also give closure to one set of tasks and set the stage for what's coming next, and they reinforce the idea of progress in the minds of employees.

Celebrations can be a bit more formal than just having a quick bite of cake and going back to work. Celebrations can be organized with an agenda of activities. If you are acknowledging a big success by an individual or a small group within a larger organization, you can make a very short speech recognizing what was done, why it was worthy of a celebration, and how it contributed to the organization's mission and goals. Celebrations may include the presentation of a plaque or other formalized statement of achievement.

Hint: Some people love celebration and some don't. Set free your employees who really love celebration, and they will organize some superb events for you.

In a formal, organized celebration of success, use the opportunity to wander around in a relaxed setting and talk with your staff. Make a point to single out those being acknowledged and chat briefly with them. As busy as you are, your presence and attention is reward in itself. A celebration can be an opportunity for you to reinforce desirable behaviors, either formally in a short speech tailored to the occasion or informally as you talk with employees.

Guidelines on Celebrating Success

- The scope of the celebration should match the achievement.
- Give of yourself (your time, your attention) to as many of those present as possible.
- View the celebration as another activity to improve the cohesion of teams and the organization.
- Clearly acknowledge what is being celebrated and how it relates to the organization's goals.
- Don't be predictable—have something besides a sheet cake with vanilla icing.
- Have fun!

Do

Define outcomes

How long did it take?

How much did it cost?

What is the short-term profit impact?

What is the long-term profit potential?

How does this outcome compare to forecasts?

How does this change compare to previous performance?

An "outcome measure" is an indication of progress toward achieving an organizational objective, such as putting a new process in place to reduce errors or adding a new product to your line. Establish outcome measures before you begin execution; that way you'll know how to meaningfully measure your progress. If you implement practices or make changes to existing procedures without thinking through what you expect to accomplish, you will never know if you have succeeded. And if you don't put intermediate outcome measures along the path toward your goals, you may find out too late that you have made a wrong turn.

Define outcomes along several dimensions, including time, cost, quality, profitability, benefits, actions, and reactions. You can't improve what you can't measure, so your outcome measures must be quantifiable. For product-oriented businesses, quantifying outcomes can be fairly straightforward.

In service or nonprofit organizations (NPOs), it is possible, but a bit more challenging, to define outcome measures. For example, an NPO can elect to evaluate how well it is accomplishing its program goals as judged by percentages from 0 to 100 percent. They can look at efficiency as a function of cost per unit served, or they can use the general and administrative cost measured against overall budgets or direct-service funding.

An NPO's defined outcomes can look at a program's impact, for example, of all known X, what percent has been served. (The Urban Institute developed a concept and methodology for measuring NPO's that is referenced in Further Reading.)

EXERCISES

Exercise 1
Identifying Outcome Measures

A new product released six months ago has not had the sales you expected. What outcomes measures would you initiate to understand the current situation and improve sales?

List of Outcome Measures

Outcome measure	Data to be collected	Time schedule to collect data

How would you use this data?

Exercise 2
Offering Help

Thinking across the last year, can you list an opportunity you took to offer help? What happened?

Were there opportunities to offer help that you missed? What were they?

Long-term Effects of Acting with Accountability

Describe the situation in which you offered help and the outcome for you and the employee.

_____

_____

Describe a missed opportunity to offer help. How can you do better in this area?

_____

_____

IMPROVE

Introduction

Great organizations have a passion to become even better, and they act on it. Traditional organizations may be dissatisfied with the status quo but fail to constantly improve. There is room for improvement in any organization. To look back and see increased efficiency, more effective processes, better employee morale, and a tight, well-oiled organization is rewarding for you and your employees. To do that, good improvement efforts are based on current performance data linked with needs of internal and external customers. Remember, your employees are your internal customers.

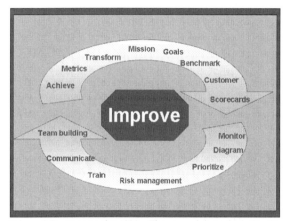

To improve, your organization must change in little and sometimes big ways. Change requires a commitment from senior management, a clear idea of where you are and where you want to go, communication with employees, training, and feedback. There are several improvement models, often called quality programs, based on adaptation and enhancement to the core work done by Walter Shewhart in the 1920s and his later co-worker Edward Deming in the 1930s. These models include Six Sigma, Kaisen, and Lean Sigma among others.

Warning: These models are not ends, only means. The model is only a tool for improvement. Organizations that think the model is the answer always fail at improvement and then blame the model.

The common themes in these approaches to improving quality include the following:

- It is essential to understand customers' real requirements.

- Measurement is the key to improvement.
- The cornerstone of your organization's success is customer satisfaction.
- You succeed through people. Your teams should operate in harmony with your organization's mission and constantly seek better ways to meet customer's needs.
- Improvement is an iterative process.

Chapter 9: Self Improve

In the introduction to this workbook, the three basic tasks of effective leadership and management were identified: inspire, improve, and implement. Improvement begins with improving yourself.

A program of self-improvement will make you a better manager and a more successful leader. Hunger for learning is a common trait among great leaders; they are committed to the process of self-improvement.

After you finish school and master your first job, your learning journey is not complete—it's just beginning. It is exciting and enriching to place yourself in situations where you are always learning something new or refining your knowledge and capabilities. When you commit to continual, personal improvement as a way of life, you will find increased satisfaction in everyday activities and a career that is continuously fulfilling.

The grist for the mill of self-improvement comes from many sources—other people, new experiences, course work, and reading. Once you decide to accept continual learning as part of self-improvement, you will seek out those experiences and individuals that will help you make yourself a more knowledgeable manager and leader.

What you will learn in this chapter:

The benefit of taking classes
- Where to find useful classes or workshops
- What classes should you take

Reading —another effective learning strategy
- Finding useful books
- Getting and keeping instructional information

Growth by stretching
- What is a stretch job
- How you and the organization benefit from stretching

Learning from peers and subordinates
- Why you should seek out learning opportunities from peers and subordinates
- How you can get the most from interactions with peers and subordinates

Cw

Take leadership courses and workshops

Why should you take a course or attend a workshop in addition to learning on the job? On-the-job learning is useful but is unstructured and subject to the vagaries of chance. Courses and workshops teach specific skills through lectures, exercises, and feedback on key elements of leadership, and are often taught by people who have been successful leaders. Courses and workshops promote learning skills that you can generalize to a broad array of situations.

Another significant advantage of taking a class or attending a workshop is stepping away from the minute-to-minute distractions that characterize the work environment. It lets you recharge your batteries. You have time and permission to focus on what is being said and to think about what you are doing and how well you are doing it. There is another subtle effect at play in taking courses and workshops—cognitive dissonance. If you pay for something with time or money, you tend to value it more highly.

Because you will be spending your valuable time and money, you want to ensure you take courses and workshops that are useful. First, get recommendations from others in your organization or peer group. Chances are if they found the content and presentation useful, so will you. Second, seek recommendations from professionals through publications or news articles—not advertisements but reviews and comments the contributors make about a course or workshop. Here are some other sources for finding effective courses and workshops:

Finding Effective Leadership Courses and Workshops

- Research blogs and articles by professionals in your area.
- Attend courses and workshops given by authors you respect and admire.
- Investigate weekend courses and seminars offered by local universities or community colleges.
- Network with your professional contacts for their recommendations.
- Read feedback from others who have taken a course—available online for many classes and workshops.
- Contact state or federal regulatory agencies that deal with leadership issues, and ask about training programs and seminars in your area.

45

Ba

Read books and articles

Make a list of books to read.

Always have reading material with you.

Ask others for reading suggestions.

Set aside time for reading.

There are always more books and articles to read.

The wealth of ideas and knowledge available through books and articles is limitless. Because there are thousands of books and articles to choose from, you may be overwhelmed with options. Our knowledge of leadership is expanding because of advances in positive psychology, brain theory, and scientific polling. For example, to learn *what* motivates employees, read *First Break all the Rules* by Curt Cunningham and Marcus Buckingham—it is based on an in-depth Gallup study. Then to learn *why* employees are motivated, delve into the human brain with *What Happy Companies Know* by Dan Baker, Cathy Greenberg, and Collins Hemingway.

You also want to catch a twentieth-century classic like Peter Drucker's 1954 *The Practice of Management,* or read anything about the genius George Catlett Marshal and how he organized resources in World War II. But also consider three other categories:

First, checkout publications in your industry and profession. Select solid, peer-reviewed publications that provide information on state-of-the-art techniques and best practices.

Second, select books by or about people you admire. Often, as a corporate icon slows down their business commitments, they feel compelled to write a "what I learned along the way" book.

Third, go far afield. Don't limit your reading to just your profession or business area. Some of the most creative ideas and solutions may come from entirely different fields since management and leadership challenges are not unique to one area. For example, Ben Rich's *Skunkworks: A Personal Memoir of My Years at Lockheed* is a story of creativity and courage.

Because you will gain many ideas and learn useful material through reading, you need a strategy to organize and retrieve information contained in written materials. Pretend you are in school—you should take advantage of highlighting and marking interesting concepts. Beyond that, you may consider tagging the front of a document or flagging pages with memorable content. Although summarizing content or keeping indexed files by subject is very useful, most people do not have the time to systematically apply this strategy.

One thing you should do when you find really useful and provocative writing is to share it. Alerting others in your peer group or management chain to books and articles of interest will increase corporate memory and improve the chance that you will find a piece of data or a useful example when you need it later.

Job stretch encompasses activities that demonstrate what you can do on a larger stage: possibly a job with a bigger operating budget, greater complexity, more challenges, or more employees to supervise. A stretch job is one that challenges you to learn new skills and take risks—in other words, to get out of your comfort zone. Why would you want to do that? Because it can be invigorating and sharpen you to be a better manager and leader. (See some examples of stretching in the box below.)

Job stretching benefits you and your organization. You gain a new perspective that will improve your decision making. You will know more about your organization, and you will learn about the challenges on the other side of the wall such as, why marketing oversells a product that is demonstrably useful as it is, why R&D creates products that are difficult to make in large quantities, what goes on in budgeting, and where the money comes from.

Additionally, your company benefits from having more well-rounded managers who are able to step into many roles, and you personally benefit because learning new things can be fun, you will get to know other people in your organization in a more personal way, and you will have a whole new set of skills should you need to move on or up.

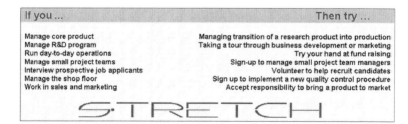

If you ...	Then try ...
Manage core product	Managing transition of a research product into production
Manage R&D program	Taking a tour through business development or marketing
Run day-to-day operations	Try your hand at fund raising
Manage small project teams	Sign-up to manage small project team managers
Interview prospective job applicants	Volunteer to help recruit candidates
Manage the shop floor	Sign up to implement a new quality control procedure
Work in sales and marketing	Accept responsibility to bring a product to market

S·TRETCH

Ls

Learn from peers and subordinates

Listen

Ask

Seek out

Find out

Know what you do not know

Learn to learn

Teach others

Ask for help

Learning from masters is valuable because they have a wealth of experience that can give you a leg up along the way. Another equally powerful but often untapped source of knowledge comes from your peers and subordinates. To find gold, reach out to individuals in your organization or similar organizations that have roughly the same level of responsibility as you have.

It can be mildly threatening to learn from your peers, who in some sense may also be your competitors. This tension is common in organizations that foster too much internal competition. Significant research proves this belief is mistaken.

Organizations and individuals do better when the culture is one of shared goals and mutual benefit. This is the kind of organization you want to have and to be part of. What are some effective strategies for learning from peers in your organization?

- Hold brown-bag lunches with discussions that focus on a topic of joint interest, such as a new technology, an article from a management publication, or implementing a new process.
- Accept a special project from senior management, and build a team of your peers who will work to find solutions and implement strategies — in the process of working together, you can learn from each other's skills.
- Ask for input (element 55) and feedback.

Look for peers in similar organizations who you can meet and learn from through professional organizations, seminars, and conferences. Also, do not miss out on peers in the cyber world. There are many online blogs and forums that encourage discussion about issues, challenges, and solutions in the management domain. For example, Scott Berkun, well known author of *The Art of Project Management* and *The Myths of Innovation* hosts a respected e-mail-based newsgroup for IT managers in which he presents a challenge problem each week for comment by the group. The exchanges are lively and filled with useful advice from project managers. (The news group is currently hosted by Shawn Murphy.)

Finally, don't forget your employees or subordinates. You will be amazed at what you can learn from them if you ask for their input. Not only can they tell you the *what, when, where,* and *why* about their jobs, but they also may know *how* other organizations solve problems and improve processes because of their past work experience. Subordinates may surprise you with their knowledge about the organization, technology, and management because they have read about it, studied it, and talked among themselves. There is a vast reservoir of knowledge in your subordinates you should tap for your own and the organization's advantage.

Time and money to do this can be an issue. To minimize costs, people who run small businesses can get together before the workday for a low-cost, monthly breakfast and best practices swapping.

Leaders Listen
Leaders Learn

EXERCISES

Exercise 1
Getting Useful Information from Business Articles

To making your reading experience more useful, answer these questions:

Select an article to read. You can find many useful articles on business and management at businessweek.com, for example.

1. Why did you select the article you did?

2. What useful information did you get from the article (25 words or less)?

3. What interesting, but not immediately useful, information did you get from the article?

4. Would you recommend this article to someone else? Why?

Exercise 2
Learning from Subordinates

Getting the Knowledge from Your Subordinates

Select an aspect of your business that you know little about – be creative here. For example, do you know how travel vouchers are processed? How the security of your organization's computers is maintained? The best local restaurant for Mexican food? Find out!

1. Did you get the information?
2. How did you find the person to ask?
3. What did you learn?
4. Did what you learn cause you to take any action?
5. How will you remember this new information?

Chapter 10: Solve Problems

Managers solve problems. Every enterprise has problems or challenges that require tailored solutions, short- and long-term fixes, or sudden directional changes. As a manager, your employees and stakeholders will turn to you for solutions so you need to develop and perfect your skills in solving problems.

Problem solving is best done with a disciplined process. First, learn to recognize the problem, and then define it in understandable ways. If your knowledge of the problem is confined to a sense that "something's not right," trying to solve the problem is likely to end in failure. It is essential that you can deconstruct the problem into contributing components to get at the root cause.

In understanding and solving problems, it's important to collect measurable and meaningful information that gives you deeper insight. Next, you need to objectively analyze the data—does it make sense, does it help explain the past or predict the future, and does it point the way to potential solutions? Once you have this understanding, you can begin to construct solutions that will improve processes or address the root cause of a problem.

What you will learn in this chapter:

Defining a problem so it can be solved
- Why correctly defining a problem is challenging
- Practice defining solvable problems

The importance of measurement in problem solving
- Finding the right characteristics to measure
- Defining data parameters

Systematic study of data yields insight into problem characteristics
- What data
- How much and how often should data be studied

Solving problems—implementation
- Coming up with options
- Involving stakeholders

P

Define the problem

Your problem definition should not include an implied solution.

Say: "Orders move too slowly" versus "We need a new automated process to handle orders."

Say: "We need more operating funds" versus "We need to write more grants."

"Define the problem" sounds pretty basic, but the more you get into this element, the more challenging it becomes. Element 28 seems so simple, and we tend to gloss over it. In reality, proper problem definition is crucial for a valid solution.

So when you think, "Everyone knows what the problem is," in reality, this is probably not the case. The human brain is hardwired to jump to solutions. Even experts make big mistakes and sometimes try to solve a surface issue, solve the wrong problem, or actually define the problem in terms of a solution they unconsciously accepted beforehand. Here's an example:

Noticing Mary Beth's all-out efforts on a project, a co-worker asked what she was doing. Mary Beth responded, "The problem is we don't have an employee handbook."

When asked why it was a problem, Mary Beth responded that her employees scored low on the survey section "knowing what was expected of them at work."

What went wrong here? Mary Beth confused a solution (making an employee handbook) with the problem definition (employees' uncertainty over Mary Beth's expectations). If she had defined the problem better, perhaps she could have come up with a simpler solution than writing a complete and more powerful handbook to clarify her expectations.

Whether you are in the public or private sector, clearly defining the problem first puts you on the right track to solving the problem. To define a problem, begin by writing a couple of sentences describing the problem, preferably as outcome measures that do not meet expectations. Next, write one sentence on why the problem needs to be solved (e.g., how it adversely affects accomplishing your mission or goals). Lastly, write one sentence describing the desired results. Why just a sentence for each? Because reducing and consolidating your perceptions and data into one sentence will help you get to the heart of the problem.

In really complex situations, you may need a team to flesh out the parameters of the problem. Remember, whether defining the problem is done individually or through team interactions, defining the problem is the first and most important step to solving it.

If you have a team tackling a problem, include their names and roles and the scope of the problem. This is called a team charter, and if done up front, it can avoid the countless times you've heard someone after a few weeks say, "Oh, *that's* the problem!"

Sometimes it helps sharpen your definition of the problem if you look at the situation from a customer's viewpoint, whether it's an external or internal customer. For example, a customer might view Mary Beth's employees, with their lack of job clarity, as providing unresponsive service.

A problem is also an opportunity — particularly when it comes to customers' problems — since it gives you a chance to improve your service level.

Remember, most experts say defining the problem is the hardest step. If you find yourself getting nowhere, your team gets bogged down, or solutions don't seem to work, go back to problem definition — that's probably where you went wrong.

46

Mi

Measure It

How much?
How often?
Who's affected?
Who cares?
What does it cost?

Before you can solve a problem, it is essential to define the parameters that characterize it: Is it recurring? What is the frequency, severity, and variability of the conditions? Is it a people or systemic problem?

Systemic problems are serious and may reflect a fault in routine. What is the evidence that there is a problem? Has someone reported one? Is there a negative trend in financial, personnel, or customer-satisfaction surveys? Are process outcomes different than expected? If the answer is yes, then there may be a problem. You still won't know for sure what solutions to apply until you take measurements.

. There are two type of system problem: the process does not work or the process works but is not being followed correctly. You need to know which of these statements is true before you start with measurements.

Good measurement is tricky. Consider the factors that directly affect the situation, such as timing, trends, and before and after events. You need to know how things *should* be to know when they are not that way. Look for correlations that will help pinpoint the problem in a way that allows solutions.

It's tempting to react before you have all the measurement data, but be careful—you can jump too early and end up solving the wrong problem or applying a suboptimal solution.

If you use a formal measurement device like an attitude survey, market penetration analysis, or operational observation, be certain that the data being collected is directly related to the problem. To get meaningful data, you have to measure the right things.

What can happen when you do not understand the pedigree of your data

Employees complained loudly about the customer service from neighboring Department A. A woman tasked with understanding the problem discovered employees in Department A collected satisfaction surveys, and she thought this data would give her a great start in gathering measurements. When she reviewed the surveys, however, the customers of Department A all reported 100 percent satisfaction. This result did not correlate with her observations or the comments of others. What was happening?

When she asked the man who collected the satisfaction survey data, she was told, "Oh, we throw out the bad ratings." When asked why, he said, "The reason we collect the data is so we can save the good responses because we can quote from them when we are writing up cash award requests for the Department A service team."

Example of measuring a problem: Your operations director reports that expenses are up 15 percent over last year. This seems high. You pull data for the last ten years and find that this rate of increase is significantly higher than average. You have a problem, but you have not defined the problem well enough to develop a plan to solve it. You need to collect more information to better understand the problem—you need to measure its parameters and then apply visualization (element 51) and trend analysis (element 83) in order to identify where applying solutions will be most effective.

Whether you have made a commitment to continual improvement or you have a problem to be solved, you should spend time formally understanding the parameters and components of the situation before you begin implementing a solution. Think about what happens when you bring a new toy home to your cat: The cat does not begin playing with it immediately. She studies it. She walks around it. She smells it. She may tentatively push it with her paw or nudge it with her nose. She is trying to understand what it is, what it does, and whether it is a threat.

Although intuition plays a role in understanding and planning, it should be only one of the tools you apply when studying a problem and looking for a solution. You'll gain the greatest benefit from a formal approach to studying and chronicling the events that swirl around the problem. Within the element family of Solve Problems, completing the first two elements (element 28 – Define the problem) and (element 46 – Measure it) prepared you to study or analyze the information you collect before you implement a solution (element 110). An effective strategy for systematically studying a problem is to apply visualization tools, such as process maps, Pareto charts, and cause-and-effect diagrams. (You can read about these visualization tools and process techniques in detail in elements 31, 49, and 81.)

A visualization tool populated with data helps you study the problem in an organized way. When you have completed studying the problem in a systematic way, you are better prepared to begin solving it. To illustrate, let's use a cause-and-effect diagram to study the problem of increasing transportation costs.

A cause-and-effect diagram goes by two other names: an Ishikawa diagram, after its inventor, and a fishbone diagram because of its appearance. The diagram breaks down the factors inhibiting success into main causes and contributing causes. This tools helps you study the problem and the environment in which the problem occurs.

In this case study example, you identify a problem involving increased costs in three areas of operations: utilities, benefits, and transportation. Selecting transportation, you want to understand the factors that have contributed to the increase in costs, so you collect data and study it. Here is how developing a fishbone diagram might point you in the right direction to begin decreasing transportation costs:

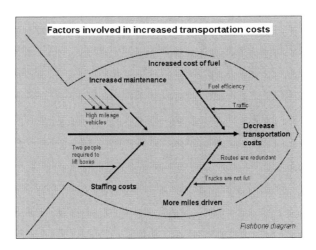

Now that you have identified some of the component problems that are driving the higher cost for transportation, you can brainstorm solutions in small, manageable bites. Perhaps you can make your boxes lighter so only one person is needed to load, transport, and deliver products. Or, you can choose to invest in route optimization algorithms to improve the load, distribution, and travel for deliveries. Remember, elaborating on the problem components places you in a better position to solve the problem of higher transportation costs than just knowing that the costs are too high.

F

Implement a solution

Brainstorm options:

Will the proposed solution work in the long term?

Are there potential, unintended consequences of the proposed solution?

What measures indicate success?

As you worked your way through the Solve Problems group of elements, you defined a problem, measured the relevant parameters, and studied and analyzed your data. Now it is time to implement a solution. You should feel secure in your ability to solve the problem because of the groundwork laid by your thorough understanding of what factors contribute to it.

Solutions to a problem are suggested by the causes you and your team have identified. Once you've picked the root cause, the proposed solution jumps out. Your solution may require straightforward changes, or it may require creativity or out-of-the-box thinking and the commitment of those individuals involved to make the solution work.

Human nature being what it is, people are more committed to making a solution work when they are part of generating that solution and when they receive credit for its success. If the problem is "office supplies are costing too much" for example, involve those who use supplies and order supplies in brainstorming possible solutions to the causes identified in element 78 (Study it). The goal of reducing the cost of supplies by 10 percent may have come from your boss, but how you get there should be the result of a team effort to identify cost drivers and saving strategies. Once you have developed a set of solutions, give credit to the team for their efforts in helping solve the problem. As you measure progress toward accomplishing your objective, give feedback on the progress being made and acknowledge the contributions of others.

A significant advantage in following the process to "implement a solution" is the real data you have to support the problem and the well-thought-out options and plans developed by your team. This commitment on your part will help persuade others who may be responsible for allocating funds or giving approval.

EXERCISES

Exercise 1
Practice with Problems

Defining the Problem

*Select one area of your business: HR,
operations, business development,
fund raising, or production. Pick an
area you know well and that needs to
improve. For the area you select, list
in detail three problems for which you
can answer these questions:*

1. What makes you think there is a problem?

2. What would be the benefit of solving the problem?

3. Where, how, and when does the problem occur?

4. Why do you think the problem is happening now?

Exercise 2
Collecting Useful Data

Using Data to Understand Problems

*For the three problems you identified
in Exercise 1, you need to identify the
data that will delineate the problem
and direct the solution.*

1. What data about the problem are available?
2. What additional data do you need?
3. What can you learn from the data?
4. How will the data change if you are successful in solving the problem?
5. How much data do you need?

Chapter 11: Customer Focus

In the final analysis, customers can make or break business. If you offer a good product that meets a customer's needs, in a fair manner you can have a successful business. If you fail to do any of those things, your business will probably not be as successful as you hoped.

Every aspect of your business, from product development through follow-up sales, needs to add value and support to your customers. This is true whether you are building picture frames, selling financial services, or treating cancer. In this chapter, we talk about the importance of meeting your customers' requirements.

Customer satisfaction extends beyond the product or service itself to include customer's experiences in interacting with your organization. If a customer complains, you listen and act to improve the situation and rectify the problem. Customer complaints should not be thought of as irritants but rather opportunities to improve.

Treat your customers and their concerns with respect, and if along the way you can add whipped cream to the product pie as a gesture of that respect and the importance you place on pleasing the customer, all the better for you and the organization.

What you will learn in this chapter:

Learning from customer complaints
- What data should you collect about complaints
- Analyzing customer complaints

Customer requirements
- Characteristics of useful requirements
- Organizing requirements

Designing with the customer in mind
- When to involve customers in design
- How to get customer feedback while there is time to make changes

Delighting the customer pays dividends
- What does it mean to delight a customer
- Organizational requirements

What about?

Unique or systemic?

How frequently?

How serious?

Who?

Solvable?

Believe it or not, complaints are a valuable resource in your quest for improvement. A complaint represents more than an outburst from a disgruntled customer — it represents useful information from someone trying to help you do better. We are predisposed to not like receiving complaints, but documenting complaints and, more specifically, measuring them in a way that provides guideposts for improvement is useful, if not essential, for your organization's future survival.

Measuring complaints is not about customer satisfaction per se. If a single customer has a complaint about a product or the outcome of a process, you should deal with that individual as soon as possible. You may choose to explain your process, compensate the customer if appropriate, or otherwise rectify the situation.

Measuring an aggregation of complaints, on the other hand, is a formal process that takes the negative performance feedback from consumers and quantifies it by abstracting the data and organizing it into categories that can lead to action.

By tracking and categorizing complaint information, you can look for trends in the data, gauge the severity or risk associated with the complaints, and perhaps prevent or limit them in the future. Simply counting complaints will not adequately reflect the nature or risk of a problem. Instead, you should monitor across four dimensions: frequency, customer characteristics, event characteristics, and type of issue (e.g., service, product, or process).

Next, apply analysis and visualization techniques to the data. Once you've characterized the complaint data by geographic location, time, customer characteristics, type of complaint, and severity of complaint, you can determine if the complaint is driven by systemic problems or was an isolated instance. (Hint: in most cases, it's systemic.)

One other comment about collecting complaint information — research shows customers appreciate a chance to tell you what they are complaining about in their own words. Offering free-form text input, in addition to check boxes or numerical evaluations, presents a challenge to data analysis and visualization, but the free-form data is valuable. To use free-form input, however, someone must take the time to extract data from the text and represent that data in the analysis process.

After you have organized and analyzed complaints, you can decide what to do differently. For example, you can perform trade-off analysis for costs and benefits of proposed changes or develop a response plan. Remember; continue to monitor complaints after you take corrective action to ascertain whether the actions changed the complaints.

Below is an example of analyzing complaint data collected by a fictitious university about the class enrollment process. Your goal as the university administrator is to reduce complaints. However, you need to understand what students are complaining about, determine which of the complaint issues can be addressed, and then prioritize your action plans. Looking at the four essential elements of complaint data analysis you find.

- Frequency = the number of complaints by category
- Customer characteristics = students enrolling in classes
- Event characteristics = steps in enrollment and the environment
- Type of issue = the category of complaint (If you do not understand the complaint from the category, then you should add detail to the item to improve your understanding.)

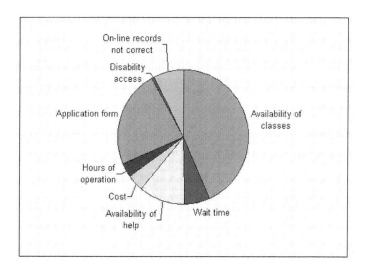

Student Complaint Frequency by Category

Kr

Determine key, customer requirements

Concise?

Attainable?

Complete?

Consistent?

Unambiguous?

Verifiable?

Dependencies?

Necessary versus desirable?

When?

How much?

Constraints?

How fast?

It's crucial to focus on two types of customers:

- External customers who rely on you to have their requirements met.

- Internal customers—employees who depend on other employees to perform needed services so they can do their jobs.

Most of this discussion deals with the first type of customer, but remember, determining the key, customer requirements of the internal customer is crucial for process improvement, employee morale, and organizational performance.

All organizations have a common need to work successfully with customers, and all can do a better job of getting and maintaining customers when they find the real customer requirements.

Some customers and potential customers explicitly tell you what their needs are, but more often, they tell you in a rather confused way. It's your task to understand their operating environment, possibilities, and goals to show them how you can meet their needs. To decode what the customer really wants, study the chart below to see how it often takes close but polite questioning to go from vague outbursts to feasible, clear, and correct requirements

Customer says:	Customer is thinking:	Customer means:	You gather data:
"You screwed up my delivery!"	My order was late!	The order arrived three days after I expected.	Fifty-five percent of our shipments miss customer delivery expectations.

Reminder: Remember those important internal customers (employees) we mentioned above? In both the private and public sector, employees frequently suffer in silence. When they do speak out, they are prone to state key requirements in an even more ambiguous way than external customers.

Now we get to the most important part of element 47—key customer requirements. Those are the customer requirements that will be most influential in the customer's decision making. Your customer may want to purchase a car that

- runs well
- is fast
- is stylish
- gets good gas mileage
- is safe
- is affordable

But how does the customer rank the relative importance of each of these requirements? The high priority items are the "key" requirements.

In software development, there is a saying: "software can be fast, cheap, or user friendly—pick two." You can't meet all customer requirements, so you must select and understand their key requirements and meet those.

Case study: The U.S. Social Security Administration analyzed key customer requirements for the burgeoning retirement wave. As a result, they redeployed staff personnel and pushed more information out through e-government initiatives. They incorporated performance measures to track projected baby boomer retirements and compared those measures to Social Security performance goals.

To understand key customer requirements, carefully probe and listen to current and potential customers. Validate your list by reiterating to the customer what you think they said. You can help your customers refine their requirements through interviews, focus groups, or checklists.

After you have a list you and the customer are comfortable with, prioritize it. Review this with the members of your staff who have the closest contact with the customers and make a final check by seeing if the key requirements explain other customer complaints you've measured (element 29).

Warning: Customers do not always know their requirements.

Understanding customer requirements significantly improves processes and helps accomplish your business objectives. For example, a key area of customer requirement is often time. It is crucial to consider and measure time when tailoring and aligning your processes to your customers' key requirements. How much time is realistically acceptable to the customer for you to perform each step? When you schedule a set of tasks, use their required total cycle time as a constraint. Then improve each scheduled task against the required cycle time. The result will be happier customers.

Tip: This is not a one-shot approach. Continually probe for shifting or missing key customer requirements to further improve the process you just designed. For example, you offer a financial planning service, and your ideal customer demographic is someone with a job, a commitment to lower personal debt, and a desire to begin saving. By continually digging for additional customer requirements, you find it is often difficult for customers to find a time to meet with you. Why? They are likely to be working while you are open — Monday through Friday from 8:00 AM until 5:00 PM. So you modify your process by making office hours more convenient to the customer's schedule.

Profit in business comes from repeat customers, customers that boast about your project or service, and that bring friends with them.[xxiv]
—W. Edward Deming

Deep dive: What if you want to do more than merely refine an existing process? Another way you can involve customers in the design process is through prototyping. Let's say your customer requires a software tool to test updates to their Web site. Per element 47, you involved the customer directly in establishing requirements for the software tool. You considered and prioritized the customer's requirements into your design. But often, customers don't articulate or even know all of their needs until they begin using your product or service; you don't find out about their unidentified needs until they complain about your product or service. Building a prototype and gaining customer participation in testing gives you an opportunity to further define requirements when changes are less costly.

"The question is, then, do we try to make things easy on ourselves or do we try to make things easy on our customers, whoever they may be?"[xxv]
—Niccolo Machiavelli

In summary: You will always be more successful when you consider the sometimes hidden needs and preferences of your customers when designing a process. It's easy to measure when you've done a good job — sales and profit increase, you get more positive, external evaluations, and you see reductions in complaints.

De

Delight the customer

You delight a customer when you do something so unexpected that they smile, say thank you, and perhaps become customers for life. Delighting a customer goes a step beyond pleasing them because the customer carries a strong memory of the event. A delighted customer knows you did something special just for them — it had personal impact. Here is an example of turning a mistake into a delight from Tom Turrentine[xxvi].

> "During a press check for a high-end annual report, the customer noticed the wrong paper stock had been special ordered from the mill. There wasn't time to reorder because the job had to be delivered in three days. Tom had an upset customer on his hands. Rather than panic or make excuses, he apologized immediately and remained calm as he started searching for solutions. When he offered to add varnish or run 100 extra copies, the customer lit up with delight. It turns out the customer wanted varnish but had not been able to stretch the budget to include it. The account representative thanked the customer for being understanding and patient, and the customer thanked the account representative for turning what looked like a disaster into a windfall."

In order to practice "delighting customers," it is essential to have an organizational philosophy and structure that supports such behavior. To teach "delighting the customer" to your employees, you must model it and allow your employees to make on-the-spot decisions that will add value to a deal or solve a problem for a customer because immediacy is critical.

At the Ritz Carlton, housekeepers have a five-thousand-dollar budget authority to solve customer complaints on the spot. That's a lot of authority, but they use it responsibly. If, in the printing example, the account representative had had to check with several layers of management to offer costly varnish to the customer's print job, the delay in solving the problem is likely to have removed any positive value inherent in the offer.

EXERCISES

Exercise 1
Customer Requirements

Using a Form to Collect Customer Requirements

Getting and documenting customer requirements can be challenging, so it helps to create a form with the parameters you need. Think about a future activity, like creating a new product or writing a proposal – what parameters should be collected from potential customers to ensure that you product meets requirements?

1. What is the end product?

2. What customer problem does the product solve?

3. What are the detailed characteristics required (how much, how fast, how expensive)?

4. How will you prove to the customer that this is the product he/she wants and needs?

Exercise 2
Delighting the Customer

What can you do to further delight your customers?

Think about a product or service you offer – list three things you could do to delight your customers about this product. Why are you not doing them?

_____

_____

_____

Chapter 12: Push the Envelope

Leading and managing a successful business venture or a nonprofit organization involves trade-offs because you want more than you have time or resource to achieve. But prudent risk taking can help you accomplish more than you otherwise might by pushing the envelope of your capabilities, ideas, and creativity.

Effective leaders and managers acknowledge and manage risk. They increase the possibility of success because they involve their employees in the planning and decision-making process; they reward intelligent risk taking and avoid punishing failure. Leaders practice due diligence and collect status information with the long-term goal of moving the organization forward.

You are not alone. Within your organization are talented people with great ideas waiting for a chance to try them out. Your job is to support those employee ideas with resources and encouragement. Avoid punishing those who risk trying something new, even if their efforts fail to achieve the objective.

What you will learn in this chapter:

The importance of setting priorities
- Comparing tasks as a function of priority
- Communicating priorities

Employee involvement is essential
- Why get employees involved in setting goals and fixing problems
- What not to do

Why you must take risks
- Identifying risks
- Managing risks

How mistakes can help
- Creating an environment that does not punish mistakes
- Learning from and using mistakes

Impact on long-term goals

Urgency

Dependencies

Risks

Consequences of failure

It should come as no surprise that there are often more tasks and opportunities than you and your staff has time to do. You've established the mission and vision for your organization, so now it's time to take the lead in setting priorities. Prioritization is the way you and your employees allocate time and talent among competing options. Remember, every task cannot be a number-one priority.

You set priorities as you plan and execute each day's tasks by focusing on key customer relationships, finishing one project before others, and ordering your day-to-day challenges. As a manager and leader, you establish organizational priorities and provide guidance to everyone down the chain of command who must also rack and stack their tasks each day. It's a way to clarify expectations for employees, and studies show that's critical for improved employee performance.

Hint: In building your prioritization list, competing tasks should be ranked based on analysis of several factors, including complexity (how hard is this task to do?), potential benefit of successfully completing the task, the level of risk both in completing and not completing the task, dependence on other prioritized tasks, and "do-ability" (can this task be done on time with the available resources and capabilities). Tasks with many co-dependencies, or that directly affect meeting organization missions and goals, should have a higher priority than other tasks.

Ensuring that everyone in the organization knows what the priorities are and how their performance impacts accomplishing prioritized tasks is critical to organizational performance. Therefore, you must solicit feedback from those who will be involved in task execution to understand their perception of the level of effort and difficulty as well as their knowledge about task dependencies. Just because you believe a highly prioritized task will require little effort, you may learn from your staff that the task is very difficult to accomplish because of those hidden dependencies.

Finally, setting priorities is not a static process. Plan to review priorities routinely, make changes as indicated from new information or feedback, and communicate the revisions to all concerned.

In

Get employees involved

Identify obstacles together

Brainstorm options

Ask for suggestions and comments

Recognize employee contributions

Employee involvement is not an activity—it is a leadership strategy. Use employees' operational knowledge to improve your decisions, to successfully implement objectives, and to encourage commitment to the goals of the organization.

Whether or not you get employees involved is a leadership litmus test because some managers gravitate toward autocratic control, and studies show control doesn't produce the significant employee performance that employee engagement does. As a leader and manager, either you believe in getting employees involved or you don't. If you don't believe in it, don't fake it because faking it won't work.

Weak leaders can continue as they have been—getting mediocre results by making all the decisions and telling everyone else how to do their jobs. However, leaders of successful organizations don't agree with this approach; they want and value employee involvement.

Why Do You Want Employee Involvement?

- Employees are closer to the action than you are and may see problems and solutions you don't.
- Being part of solving a problem increases an employee's commitment to successful implementation of solutions.
- In many cases, groups working together on new ideas and problems have more unique and creative solutions than any individual.
- Employees who are involved feel valued. When an employee feels valued, he or she is more likely to stay and help.

How Can You Facilitate Employee Involvement?

- You describe the need in general terms without suggesting the solution.
- You listen (see element 21) without judgment to new ideas or an employee's perception of a problem or solution.
- You provide a time line and an estimate of resources that can be applied.
- You honestly consider employee ideas—don't inadvertently send the message that this is simply an exercise, and you are going to do what you want to anyway.
- Give feedback. Explain why you agree or disagree and implement what you can.

What Can Go Wrong?

- Biasing the results by suggesting a solution before the employees consider options
- Not listening because your mind is already made up
- Using your position to take over the discussion or activity
- Setting up employee involvement as a separate activity, not part of business as usual
- Punishing midlevel managers for not making all the decisions and "just getting on with it"
- Punishing an employee for a naïve idea
- Failing to expect employee involvement

Everyone has something to contribute
- so make sure they do!

R

Take risks

We take risks everyday: commuting to the office, eating at a fast food restaurant, or accepting a blind date. Risks are a part of life, and taking risks is the way you move your organization forward. Risk means committing resources to a task without being assured of success. If you wait for less ambiguity and better definition, you may be too late to take any action at all.

Some "bet-the-company-type" risks have been well documented, like IBM's commitment to the IBM360 in the 1960s, Microsoft's decision to use the DOS operating system in the 1970s, or Apple's Macintosh computer in the 1980s. But in the normal course of your day, you will be taking smaller risks. Taking risks signals to your employees that you believe in them and their ability. Your willingness to take calculated risks emboldens employees to take risks to be successful in reaching their part of the organization's goals. We now know that organizations that promote low-level risk taking spur more innovation.

Hint: Risk taking shouldn't be done naively by pretending the chance of failure isn't present. Manage your risks with information, alternative plans, and, most importantly, frequent performance measurement. List known risks by creating thought scenarios of possible actions and reactions by doing the following:

- Considering the implications of various events on outcome conditions
- Creating a list of general sources of risk
- Assessing their applicability

Remember that risks can occur from within the organization, from competitive conditions, and from feckless Mother Nature.

Once you have identified the risks associated with a proposed action, rank them according to their impact should things go awry. Then set trigger points that signal something may be going off track, and when they do, implement your alternative plan to provide a safety cushion.

Avoiding risk entirely leads to organizational stagnation. Worse yet, remaining permanently fixed in the face of ever changing external conditions leads to rigidity and probable catastrophic failure.

Allow and learn from mistakes

Yellow sticky notes

Silly putty

Chocolate chip cookies

Liquid paper

Penicillin

Are you making enough mistakes?

People learn more from mistakes than easy successes. If you foster a culture that is not tolerant of mistakes, you create an inflexible, uncreative, and stagnant environment.

To learn from your mistakes, first admit a mistake occurred.

When you spot a mistake—such as a fizzled marketing initiative, a new process that doesn't improve performance, an experimental drug failure, or even a botched vacation where no one had fun— look at the steps in reverse to understand what happened. Collect data and understand the context surrounding the outcome. Mistakes can be opportunities in disguise, so once you collect data about the undesirable outcome, see what you can learn. Some mistakes are obvious, and correcting them can be as simple as reversing a decision or saying, "I'm sorry." Other mistakes require changing a complicated process or procedure. Ask yourself what you should have done differently and why.

Possibly the most famous story about a mistake is from IBM in the early 1980s after its big failure with the IBM PS Jr. Design problems led computer wags to call it the "Edsel of computers." When the line was finally dropped due to low sales, the project manager, expecting to be fired, asked his boss if he "should clean out his desk." The boss replied, "We just spent several million dollars training you. Why would we want to fire you?"[xxvii]

You don't need a formal process or written SOPs to learn from mistakes. Set an example for employees by adopting this policy for yourself. Great leaders admit mistakes and learn. Insecure and less successful leaders cover up, ignore, dismiss, or place blame elsewhere.

EXERCISES

Exercise 1

Setting Priorities

It's December 31, and you are making your organizational New Year's resolutions. Make a list of all of the opportunities and challenges in your organization – practice prioritizing your list either by yourself or with a team.

Prioritization Matrix

For each square, establish a value from 1–10:

List of opportunities and challenges	Importance	Urgency	Dependencies	Chance of success	Resource Availability
1					
2					
3					
4					
5					
6					

Exercise 2

Learning from Mistakes

For this exercise, pick some mistakes from your childhood or adolescence. The list you made here is a great source of powerful stories – people learn a great deal from stories of personal failures, and stories like this make you more human.

"To err is human ... "

What was the mistake?

What did you learn and how did that change your behavior as a manager and leader?

Chapter 13: Use Tools

Introduction: The ability to use tools distinguishes man from most animals. Tools extend reach and increase power. Put together the tools and information-visualization techniques discussed in this chapter, and you have a powerful force for influencing others and making decisions. In this chapter, we consider several tools that help managers understand situations, solve problems, and improve processes.

The tools described in this chapter may use visualization software, such as Excel, PowerPoint, or Visio, but many visualization techniques can be done with pencil and paper. The important point is that you need data and you need to present that data in such a way to make your understanding of the implications almost intuitive.

As a leader and manager, your goal is to improve the performance of the organization—continually. Collecting data is essential to knowing if you are meeting your goals and to spotting bumps in the road ahead. Process and visualization tools help you do your job faster and better and help you sell your solutions up the chain of command.

What you will learn in this chapter:

Why collect data
- What kind of data you should collect
- How to plan for and collect data

How you win with "why" questions
- How people use "why" questions
- What you can learn from the answers

How process mapping helps
- Building process maps
- What are swim-lane maps

Cause-and-effect or fishbone diagrams
- What are the components of a fishbone diagram
- How to build a fishbone diagram

Using Pareto charts
- What types of problems benefit from analysis with Pareto charts
- Making a Pareto chart

Learning more about control charts

Da

Data collection plan

To collect meaningful data, plan in advance what data you really need. Some people mistakenly collect data for the sake of collection rather than for understanding. You need data to help explain the root causes of the problem and to measure progress in reaching objectives. A data-collection plan should be a formalized plan reflecting your commitment to continual improvement.

Data Collection Plan Basic Questions

- What data will be collected
- How will the data be collected
- Who is responsible for collecting the data
- When will you collect data
- Why do you need this data
- How much data do you need

How much?

How often?

Where?

When?

Who?

To create a data-collection plan, start with a small project or work within one department or function. Build your plan, collect and analyze the data, and then represent that data in your planning and decision making. Element 7 (Collect data) has some suggested data points that you can use:

- Financial—costs, including raw materials, labor hours, equipment, facilities, profitability, and planed versus actual costs.
- Customer satisfaction—assessment tools like short surveys that measure satisfaction with the product or service, timeliness, and responsiveness. Also complaints and customer retention.
- Business processes—errors or defects, compliance with standards, reliability and validity, cycle time, and schedule compliance.
- Business goals—market share, proposals won, quality, diversity, and new products introduced.

Oops: A consultant working with a group that made airline reservations for thousands of other employees was delighted to learn that the group collected rating comments from each customer—it would give her insight into the bad service the group reportedly provided and save her from having to distribute a customer-satisfaction survey across the organization. When she looked in the ratings file, it was empty except for eight "Superior" comments. She asked about it and was told, "We save the good comments to write up our performance awards. We just throw away all the bad ones."

To avoid making a mistake like that and to help decide which data to collect, ask the following:

"What do I need to know to make a commitment to change something or realign resources?"

"What would I like to know before making this change?"

A data-collection plan is formal. It needs to be written down with established parameters and shared with everyone involved. Evaluate your plan and make changes as needed to maintain relevance.

You can use any number of visualization and organization tools to represent your data-collection plan. Below is one example using a Gantt chart to show the plan for collecting data on "Improving Customer Satisfaction."

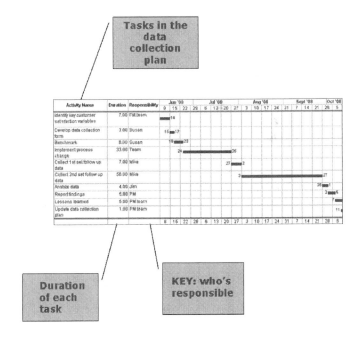

*When you ask why five
times, you can often
get to the root cause of
the problem.*

A good newspaper story answers five questions: who, what, when, where, and why. The first four provide facts that can be answered in just a few words. But "why" provides the meaning behind the facts. "Why" is very powerful, as many three-year-olds, who may send their parents near the edge, know. Young children ask why over and over again because the first answer rarely is the entire story. There is more information to be had, so they ask again.

As a manager and leader, you should use "why" to help you understand the status of a product or project, the rationale for a plan, and the thinking behind a process or an idea. "Why do you do that?" "Why do you do it that way?" "Why do you think that will work (or not)?" Many times by asking "why," you help others better understand and articulate their intuitive reasoning or tacit knowledge.

One caution about asking a "why" question—it can be a double-edged sword. If you ask why, implying disbelief or disapproval (e.g. "Why in the heck do you do that?"), the responder may become defensive or entrenched in their view. Instead, ask in a way that shows genuine, nonjudgmental interest in the answer.

Why questions should also be part of your process development and continual improvement programs. Objectively asking why a step in the process is necessary or why a strategy will work drives others into deeper thinking. *Telling* never works as well as *questioning* because questions engage the mind. This is how you push your organization to world-class levels.

Here is an example between a marketer and a manager about a new advertising campaign:

Employee: "I think we should use an animal in the marketing brochure."
Manager: "Why"?
Employee: "Animals help sell things."
Manager: "Why"?
Employee: "Animal pictures are eye-catching."
Manager: "Why"?
Employee: "People like animals, they have animals, they can relate to animals, pictures of animals are not threatening, and animals are visually interesting."

With only four why questions you have richer information to make a decision. The employee may not consciously know why he or she wanted to use an animal in the brochure, but as he or she reflected on your questions, you both learned there were several, valid reasons below the surface.

Process mapping gives a visual representation of a manufacturing product, a piece of paper, or individual as it moves through a process. A good process map allows those unfamiliar with the process to understand the workflow. Process mapping is an extremely useful technique in understanding how your business gets things done. It helps in training new employees and in looking for process improvements.

Characteristics of an efficient process:

- *Decision at lowest level*
- *Natural order of steps*
- *When and where it makes sense*
- *Single point of contact*
- *Limit backward movement*
- *Fewest steps*

A process map is a cross between a traditional process chart and a computer-system flowchart and offers a clear picture of what activities are carried out within a process. As with process charts, the usual approach in creating a process map is to identify the "as is" steps as the basis for further analysis. You have to know how things actually work before you can improve, and often, the way things work at the grassroots is very different than you think.

Process mapping can also be used to represent future processes you want to put in place. You can study workflows from every angle: responsiveness, applicability, efficiency, and cost.

Process maps can be high-level representations, as shown below, or they can be detailed. Choose the level of representation appropriate to the actions being contemplated. Here, for example, is a thirty-thousand-foot process map view of the promulgating standards process for the U.S. Army.

Here is an example of a detailed process map that helps you understand where slight changes for continual improvement could be made to improve responsiveness:

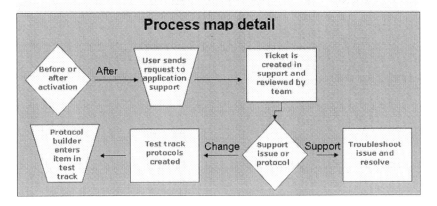

Process map detail

Process maps are visual representations of flow to help viewers "see" what is happening. Process mapping can be aided by software tools that produce graphic representations. You can use fairly simple tools like Power Point and Visio, which are probably already available in your office. However, if you are process mapping a very complex process, you may want to employ trained individuals who use specialty mapping tools tailored to specific industries and organizations.

A useful variant in processing mapping is called Swim Lane Diagrams. Swim Lane diagrams are essentially process maps with additional information about responsible people and points of interaction.

Swim Lane Process Diagram

Management	RFP released	→ Concept		Review and comment	
Tech. Staff			Text → Draft	Modify	
Support			Graphic artists		Edit and ship

49

Fb

Fishbone diagram

The cause-and-effect diagram is also known as the "fishbone" or "Ishikawa" diagram after its creator Kaoru Ishikawa. It's used to systematically list causes attributed to a specific problem (or effect). This is another visualization method that requires collecting information and representing it visually. The fishbone diagram technique is extremely powerful in helping look at the cause(s) of problems in a very complex process.

When you apply the fishbone technique to business problems, the possible causes are usually classified into six categories. You can choose other categories if some do not apply to the problem:

- Method

- Man

- Management
- Measurement
- Material
- Machine

Each of these categories is placed with an arrow along a path toward the problem, cause, or goal state. A basic chart ready to have information added would look like this:

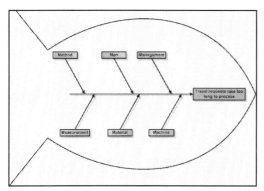

The next step in building a fishbone diagram is to brainstorm with your team the primary, secondary, and tertiary causes for the problem in each of the six categories. It may be easier to begin with the major causes followed by secondary ones. If it seems difficult to settle on just a few primary causes, it can be helpful to place a value or rank each identified cause. Then only choose the top four to six ranked causes as primary.

Each of the major causes is presented as a bone in the diagram, with the secondary causes as "bonelets." In the example below, there were complaints about a call-in help line. To identify possible causes for the perceived delays, first get more information about the types of problems reported. The staff reported issues including wait times, follow-up, communication, and failure to answer the customer's questions—these are the parameters of the problem. For each parameter, the team

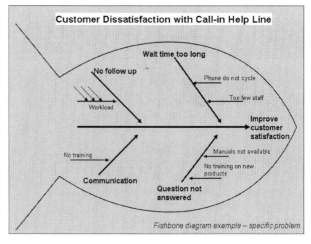

should then brainstorm causes, as shown in the diagram.

A Pareto chart is a bar graph used to summarize and display the relative differences between groups of data. In most cases, Pareto charts are used to graph problem causes. The Pareto chart is based on the principle that when several factors affect a situation, a few factors will account for most of the impact, and those is the first problems you should fix.

The Pareto principle is named after Italian economist Vilfredo Pareto, who theorized that for many situations 80 percent of variance, can be explained by 20 percent of the causes. In other words, a few things cause the bulk of your problems. Generally it is best to focus your efforts on those few factors that will most directly impact outcome.

Tip: Pareto charts are excellent for convincing others about what needs to be done first.

A Pareto chart helps teams focus on the few, really important problems or causes of problems. Comparing before and after Pareto charts is a good way to see whether an implemented solution reduced the relative frequency or cost of the original problem.

Let's look at a simple example: Your team is tasked with putting out the company newsletter each month. You find that you are always bumping up against deadlines. You are frequently late, and your team has to work overtime to get out the newsletter.

You brainstorm with the team about problems they are having and how often they occur. The team comes up with a list of seven issues that cause delays.

Category	%	Cum
Other tasks are prioritized higher	49%	49%
Articles need editing	26%	55%
Articles need to be rewritten	18%	73%
Articles are late	15%	88%
Supplies not available	5%	93%
Staff on vacation	5%	98%
Computers down	2%	100%

Using a simple chart in Excel, you see three of the problems account for over 70 percent of the delays: other prioritized tasks, articles need editing, and article need to be rewritten. Now you are in a better position to reduce the problem by attacking the two main causes. Sometimes you will use more than one Pareto chart. For example, if your first analysis shows one cause is complex or contains many variables, you may want to analyze that cause with the same Pareto methods.

Use a Pareto chart when there are many problem causes and you need to focus on the most significant ones first. Remember, Pareto charts are very useful in communicating to others the causes of problems and prioritizing solution-oriented activities.

Have you ever seen a process you thought was fixed revert back to its broken state? A control chart can help monitor variations in any repetitive process. It is one of the seven, basic, statistical tools often used in Six Sigma (Six Sigma uses benchmarking and data collection applied directly to processes), along with the Pareto Chart, histogram, check sheet, cause-and-effect diagram, flowchart, and scatter diagram. Also known as the Shewhard chart, a control chart monitors processes and assures that they remain stable.

Advanced: The control chart is a process-behavior chart that uses the process mean (average) and standard deviations to determine whether process execution is falling within an expected range of behavior or is out of statistical control.

You might use a control chart to measure time, cost, defects, errors, or quantities of things, like sales and inventory. Every control chart has three fundamental elements that can be identified: a centerline or the mathematical mean of all the samples plotted, upper and lower control limits that show and set limits on variations, and the data plotted over time. The closer variations fall to the mathematical mean, the more in control the process. Any value above or below those lines is considered to be out of control.

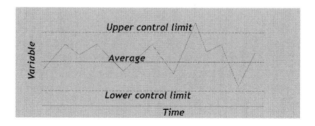

EXERCISES

Exercise 1
Data Collection

Pick a project you are working on or plan to work on – it can be personal, like adding a room to your home, or business related. Identify the data you need to plan, and assess the progress for your project.

What data will you collect and how will you visually represent it?

What data will you collect? When? How?

Is there a process or visualization tool you can use to easily understand your data?

Exercise 2
Identifying Cause and Effect

Cause-and-effect diagrams are powerful diagnostic tools. Select a problem you are experiencing and create a fishbone diagram of primary and secondary causal events for at least four of the six fishbone categories.

Fishbone Diagram

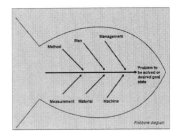

Chapter 14: Continual Improvement

Continual improvement is more than a good idea—it is an essential survival strategy. As a leader and manager, you set the organizational expectation that improving processes, products, service delivery, and customer relationships is the way you do business. Without it, you are not maximizing the potential of your organization.

Remain vigilant to opportunities to do things better and easier, starting with yourself and moving outward to every aspect of your business. The biggest driver in continual improvement is listening to your customers and the marketplace—don't forget those four elements we covered in Customer Focus (chapter 11). Be open to change, and gain ideas of what and how to improve from everyone who has a stake in your organization.

Because you have *always* done it this way does not mean that is the way you *should* do it
- Give up fixed ideas
- Understand what your organization is doing and why

How to make things happen
- Be open to new ideas
- Be a facilitator to make it happen

The value of simple solutions
- Why simple solutions may be better
- Removing complexity

Good ideas come from many sources
- How to recognize a good idea
- Test before implementation

Continual improvement is not always about spending money
- Assess long-terms costs and benefits of improvement ideas
- Sometimes continual improvement means doing less

Continual improvement is continuous
- Working cheaper, faster, and better is an iterative process
- If you are not moving forward, you are moving backward

Ab

Abandon fixed ideas

Having fixed ideas about what needs to be done and how it should be done can handicap your organization from making real improvements. For example, overly detailed, narrow job descriptions for every position and rigidly hierarchal procedures to assign, review, and execute simple tasks will cause creative rigidity. So how do you go about abandoning the fixed ideas that are impeding your progress?

Study a few of your processes systematically. For example, traveling to visit a potential customer is actually a process. List all the steps, from identifying who and when to visit, making arrangements, reporting, and reimbursing for expenses. For each major transition step, list the subtasks and identify who initiates the behavior. If approval is necessary, who does it? How is approval documented, and how long does it typically take. How do you know when the task is completed? For each identified subtask, ask yourself the following: Is this step necessary? What assumptions (managerial, behavioral, and legal) are being made? How does this step add value to the goal? There are lots of questions to ask. Don't forget the value of Asking "why" five times (element 13).

Did you notice the number of questions in the paragraph above? Asking all those questions and more is necessary to help you break through existing fixed ideas to get your organization off autopilot.

Once you begin to improve process and workflow by eliminating unnecessary steps, you improve performance and morale. Once you accept how fixed ideas, status quo, and rigid adherence to outdated approaches interfere with efficient operations, you can institute changes to vastly improve your performance.

A young girl sat in the kitchen watching her mother cut off both ends of a roast before putting it in a pan. "Why are you cutting off the ends?" she asked. "Because my mother always cut off the ends, and her roasts were delicious," replied the mother. When the little girl's grandmother came to the table that evening, the little girl asked her, "Why did you cut off the ends of the roast before you cooked it?" The grandmother replied, "Because my mother always cut off the ends, and her roasts were delicious." Still not satisfied, the little girl decided to ask her great-grandmother. The following Sunday at great-grandmother house, the girl asked, "Mom and Grandmother say they cut off the ends of a roast before they cook it because you do. Why do you do it?" "Oh," replied the great-grandmother, "because my roast pan was too short, and that was the only way to make the roast fit."

Mp

Think of ways to make it possible

A manager often finds it easier to say no than to take a risk and say "let's try it." If someone has a good idea, an "if only we could … " idea, remember that leadership is about helping others make their ideas into reality.

First, you listen. You ask yourself (with an open mind), "Does this idea make sense?" "Is the possible outcome worth the risk?" If so, calculate what it would take to make the idea happen. You will want to know:

- How much will it cost?
- Who can do it?
- How long will it take?
- Does it interfere with other projects or objectives?
- What is preventing us from doing it right now?

Does the idea require reallocating funds or reassigning staff? Do I need to remove barriers (element 42)? Do we need to make a few changes in our business as usual? In order not to dampen ardor, a CEO may ask employees to study the idea's true value added weighed against needed resources. Many employees return to kill their own idea, but their spirits weren't dampened in the process, so they continue to think up ways to "make it possible."

The unique feature of element 14 is not *what* you do nearly so much as the *attitude* of possibility you bring to the task.

32

Go

Go for simple, not perfect, solutions

Safety pin

Paperclip

The old axiom that "perfect is the enemy of good enough" can be applied to solving organizational problems. Striving for perfection can be time-consuming and immobilizing. It's usually not necessary unless you are a brain surgeon or docking the space shuttle. Element 32 has a little broader meaning than not getting caught in the search-for-perfection trap. Element 32 actively promotes seeking a simple solution. What are the characteristics of simple solutions when compared to perfect solutions?

- Simple solutions take fewer steps and resources.
- Simple solutions are easier to use.
- Simple solutions cost less.
- Simple solutions get you closer to perfection than you are now but not all the way.

Liquid paper

Duct tape

Geodesic dome

Velcro

Watch

- Simple solutions account for all necessary variables but few unnecessary ones.
- Simple solutions are elegant.
- Simple solutions are not fragile.

For example, user interfaces are frequently over-engineered. When you multiply all the choices in a typical word processing program, you have thousands of functional combinations—way too many for even an expert to remember. Skilled UI developers create hierarchies of menus and options with the simplest and most commonly used ones available on the top level.

Here's another example: Let's say you are creating a process to get approval for travel arrangements and travel reimbursement. You could make the process complex by placing oversight and signatures at each step of the process, or you could make it simple by having one step in the beginning and one step at the end. This places more responsibility on the traveler and more authority on the approvers, but the process is simple, easy to remember, and much faster.

Ironically, with fewer people involved, you have fewer mistakes—check, recheck, double, check and recheck again takes away individual responsibility. Forget this advice if you are arming a nuclear weapon—otherwise it is completely valid.

How can you go for simple solutions? First, be very clear about what is needed—not wanted or not possible—but truly needed. Next, think of ways to get what you need. For each idea or possible solution, figure out what it will cost in time, materials, and aggravation. Then select the winner. It will be the simplest solution.

50

Id

Seek ideas from many people

Once you commit to improving the way you conduct business, an almost infinite number of small improvement changes open up. It's self-defeating to try and think of everything yourself. Let's say that one more time: no matter how creative you are, you can't do this all by yourself. Nor, it seems, is asking one or two experts the most successful strategy to create a full list of new ideas. As it turns out, the best way to generate ideas that will make a difference and are likely to work in your environment is to ask the many, many people who are already there.

Ask employees for ideas. Using employee brains saved Motorola's experiment with Six Sigma in the 1980s. Once employees were engaged in the process, Motorola had more buy-in for change and the solutions were better. Employees are closest to the work and best know what is actually going on. Try out new ideas on small projects, and then implement and expand the ones that work for you.

If you want to find changes that improve productivity or workforce quality of life, ask the employees. Facilitate small group interactions of knowledgeable workers about their jobs or the company's objectives. The most powerful question you can ask the group is "why?" "Why do you do that?" "Why do you do it that way?" Once everyone understands why something is done, they are in a better position to consider and plan alternatives and improvements together.

Also consider special-interest Internet sites. There, people ask questions, present solutions, and discuss their experiences. Your goal is steady improvement, and the most effective way to get there is to seek the ideas of many knowledgeable and diverse people.

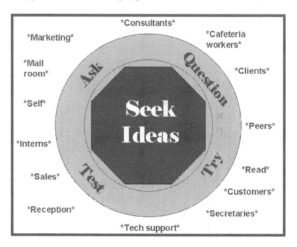

82

Ww

Use wits not wallet

The familiar axiom "work smarter, not harder" can be an irritating reminder when you are overworked, tired, and frustrated. Neuroscientists say creative thinking goes out the window when stress increases from the frenetic pace of modern life. Step back from the abyss and reflect on your situation or work tasks.

Element 82 does not suggest never spending money, but your first thoughts about how to improve performance should center on creatively attacking the problem. Think about what you want, why you want it, and how it fits in with your long-range goals and organizational mission. You need to consider if you have lower- or no-cost options that can get you to the same place.

Consider how your money is best spent. You may want new offices with your corporate name on the top of the building, but perhaps remodeling your current space will get you where you need to be. Or you may want to hire a seasoned professional for business development. Before you go looking outside for someone new, can you train and stretch someone in your organization to do the job?

Using Your Wits not Your Wallet

- Prioritize your tasks, focus, and do one thing at a time until it's finished.
- Spend most of your time on the most productive tasks.
- Learn more about the productivity tools you already have—some may solve your current challenges.
- There is no free lunch—new tools, new processes, and new people all cost time and effort in addition to money.
- Observe your co-workers, and ask questions about how they have solved a particular problem or improved performance on a set of tasks.
- Ask yourself, "does this task need to be done to help meet our goals?" If so, "does it need to be done the way we usually do it—is there a smarter, faster way?"
- Delegate—what may be a time-sink chore for you, may be an interesting challenge for someone else.
- Eliminate the unnecessary—wasted time, wasted products, and mistakes.
- Implement changes in small steps, use prototypes, and measure outcomes rather than institute sweeping changes across the board.

At the end of the day, film directors must release their movies and artists must offer their work for sale, thus ending their opportunity for further improvement. But for managers, there is no end to improving products and processes. That is a good thing. When you learn and apply what you learn to the internal workings of your organization, everyone, including your employees and customers, benefits.

Why not just make all your improvements up front? Because improvements alter the work environment, and once you make a change, the doors are open for improvements to build upon that change. Something that was not conceived of a year ago or even thought possible now becomes doable because of the first change.

The world changes too: New materials become available. Competitors change and bring small improvements or disruptive technologies to the marketplace. Employees today have different problems than those of a previous generation. The environment, no longer stable and unchanging, has become a major force in making fixed ideas (element 6) quickly obsolete. Improvement is an iterative, unending process.

The corporation best known for promoting the idea of continual improvement is Toyota Motor Corporation. A summary of "The Toyota Way" is provided in the article from the University of Michigan entitled "The 14 Principles of the Toyota Way: An Executive Summary of the Culture Behind TPS"[xxviii]. Further examples of the implementation of "The Toyota Way" are provided in Charles Fishman's article "No Satisfaction at Toyota", which describes Toyota's "insatiable competitiveness that would seem un-American were it not for all the Americans making it happen (see Further Reading). Toyota's competitiveness is quiet, internal, self-critical. It is rooted in an institutional obsession with improvement that Toyota manages to instill in each one of its workers, a pervasive lack of complacency with whatever was accomplished yesterday."

The takeaway from studying Toyota's (and other companies like Hewlett Packard, Texas Instruments, and Boeing) implementation of continual improvement is that improvement is not a process—it is an attitude that is integrated into an organization's culture.

EXERCISES

Exercise 1
Abandon Fixed Ideas

Before you can abandon fixed ideas, you must be aware of them. This exercise involves increasing your awareness. Pick a task that you know how to execute well. It can be any outcome-oriented set of tasks like making an omelet or scheduling a trip.

Increase Your Awareness of Fixed Ideas

1. Beginning with the end result and working backward, make a list of all the tasks involved reaching your objective.
2. For each task, ask yourself why you are doing that step.
3. Can you do the step differently or in a different order?
4. Could you reach the objective without some of the steps?

Exercise 2
Seek Ideas from Many People

This is an experiment. You want to get six to eight different ways to solve a problem. You can pick something personal like "raising money for a school support project" or a work related problem like "saving money on office supplies." Ask everyone you can for their ideas, and make a list.

Getting Ideas

_____

_____

_____

_____

_____

_____

For each suggestion or idea, ask yourself if you would have thought of it.

IMPLEMENT

Introduction

Implementation is where the rubber of inspiration meets the road of real business change. It is an exciting adventure to infuse your ideas and knowledge into practical changes that move your organization toward greater success. Most leaders find that implementation is the most rewarding part of their job. Implementation is converting all that theory into action and seeing the results in new customers, better returns on investment, increased market share, and greater customer and employee satisfaction.

A big challenge to implementation is the existing organizational culture. That is why you use data to make points and evaluate progress. It is also why it's necessary to involve the entire organization through communication, training, benchmarking, frequent updates, and feedback on progress. Sometimes implementation fails because:

- The approach was scattered rather than a systemic
- All levels of the organization were not involved
- Not measuring progress
- Not benchmarking the organization
- Confusing planned change with actual change

If you study and apply the core concepts embodied in Leadership & Life by the Elements, you won't make these same mistakes. In this section of the workbook, we examine how to apply fact-based decision making by collecting, analyzing, and visualizing data that provides a foundation for effective implementation.

As you reflect on the information in Section 3, along with what you absorbed in the previous sections, you will become more knowledgeable about your organization as a whole and about your people—how to gain their trust and support and how to best assess your organization's strengths, weaknesses, opportunities, and threats. You are ready to create conditions for an agile, responsive, and winning organization.

After we finish with the Implement group of elements, we will look at the Rare Earth elements in the bottom two rows of the Periodic Table of Leadership to examine attributes of the very best organizations and the keys to employee motivation. The best organizations, like those recognized by the Baldrige Award, decentralize decision making, create learning organizations, and partner in meaningful ways with employees and customers. When it comes to motivating employees, you can use the final row to make substantive improvements to ensure the future success of your organization. After all, employee performance is the major component of organizational performance.

Chapter 15: Fact-based Decision Making

Introduction: In business and organizational management, facts require data to back them up—otherwise they are just opinions. Data is a tricky entity. To have decision-supporting data, you must be selective in what data you collect and disciplined in your analysis. We are all familiar with Mark Twain's aphorism about statistics, "There are three kinds of lies: lies, damned lies and statistics."

One of the most valuable adjuncts to data analysis is data visualization. These are techniques that represent points of data in relation to one another in order to understand current status and trends more deeply and quickly. Fact-based decision making is a disciplined process that requires careful thought before processes and procedures are measured in order to collect the right data and then have unbiased, nonjudgmental analysis to extract those facts that are important in making decisions and forecasting the future.

What you will learn in this chapter:

You must have useful data to make informed decisions
- What kinds of data should you collect
- How to use basic principles of Six Sigma

Why hoarding data is bad

Selecting the most useful data to collect and analyze

Using data visualization techniques
- What is data visualization
- How data visualization aids in understanding

Trend analysis
- Anticipating the future by looking for patterns
- Techniques for trend analysis

Choosing to fix problems without blame
- Why blaming does not help
- How to address problems in order to fix them

Cd

Collect data

In order to make informed decisions and assess the impact of your actions, you must collect meaningful data. You collect benchmarking information in the beginning, and then you collect the same metrics later as the process is being executed. This comparison allows you to measure if you are making a difference and if that difference is in the right direction.

Whether your organization produces a product or provides a service, there are processes throughout that can be measured and improved. You can collect data about many variables, so it is critical that you collect data that is meaningful to the decisions you make. First, select variables that are measurable—generally that means the variable value can be reduced to a number. Second, and even more important, the variable must be a meaningful indicator of performance. Collecting the wrong data may do more harm than collecting no data at all.

Advanced: In very large manufacturing operations, a process called Six Sigma is often used as the core, data-collection process for continual improvement. Six Sigma has relatively simple, but data-intensive, measures, such as defects per million. Six Sigma uses benchmarking and data collection applied directly to processes. Don't forget, the processes you seek to measure and improve should include validation from external sources, like customer satisfaction or market share. Six Sigma measures may be difficult to apply to complex systems, low-product volumes, or service businesses. Below are some examples of data you can collect. The list is not all inclusive, of course, but it should provoke your thinking.

Data Collection Category	Types of Data You Could Collect
Financial	Costs including raw materials, labor hours, equipment, facilities, profitability, and plan versus actual costs
Customer satisfaction	Likert scales for relevant customer variables, like satisfaction with the product or service, timeliness, responsiveness, complaints, and customer retention
Business processes	Time requirements, errors or defects, compliance with external standards, reliability and validity, time from concept to product development, cycle time, inventory management, and schedule compliance
Business goals	Market share, proposals won, diversity, and new products introduced

15

Hd

Don't hoard data

You collect data to understand how your organization is doing compared to its goals and objectives. There are many reasons you might decide to keep the data to yourself, such as the power information gives you, your concern about the response to unfavorable data, your disinclination to act on the data—none of these reasons are good for your organization. Get over it. Hoarding data will result in losing credibility and trust. Continual improvement requires sharing knowledge based on comprehensive and timely data.

Sharing helps

Photo courtesy of: Liz Saunders

33

Vf

Focus on the vital few

If you collect data on many variables over any length of time, you may find yourself in the position of drowning in data and starving for information. As a manager and leader, you need to focus on the key data elements that will most directly affect your decision making. You may know already that the vital, few pieces of data include sales performance, number of complaints, increased market share, or assembly downtime, or you may not be sure which of the myriad bits of data really are vital.

You or your staff can use statistical and information visualization techniques to isolate key findings and correlate or cluster data into meaningful pieces. Your selection criteria for the "vital few" should be driven by strategic objectives.

You do not want to get too far down in the weeds of the data detail. Once you have pulled data on key indicators, your task is to select the top few, say three to five data points, and then pursue improvement of your organization's performance on those tasks. This reflects your commitment to continual improvement.

After identifying the vital few and developing objectives for future performance, work with your staff to develop tactics to reach your objectives. You need to be personally involved in monitoring performance on the vital few measures, and you need to be sure that your interest is being communicated throughout the organization.

51

Vd

Visually display data

Organizations use data to understand where they are, what is happening, and what may happen. Data help measure progress and identify problems. Data can be boring, but it doesn't have to be. Presenting data using visual representations rather than just text or columns of numbers is less boring and can communicate decision-impacting information faster. Visual representations add a dimension to the data that allows the viewer to quickly grab trends and patterns, and it is the understanding of trends and patterns that facilitates effective actions.

Presenting data visually lets you represent relationships over time, geography, and among or between groups. Well-done visualizations will make your point quickly and intuitively to your viewers, and your viewers will remember the drawn conclusions better when they can carry that visual summary around in theirs heads.

Using visualization also makes patterns apparent that might otherwise be hidden. Here is a set of examples on incidence rates. There are five different data views. Although most of them provide some information, the final one yields a pattern that can drive actions.

Region	Incidence per 100,000
1	176.82
2	167.78
3	192.48
4	162.77
5	196.26
6	195.54
7	195.20
8	208.34

Region	Incidence per 100,000
4	162.77
2	167.78
1	176.82
3	192.48
7	195.20
6	195.54
5	196.26
8	208.34

Raw data by region and raw data ordered by frequency

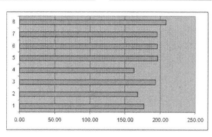

Using lines and bars to represent frequency makes a regional comparison is easier

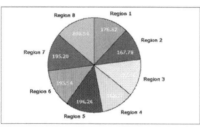

This view adds no information and makes conclusions more difficult to make

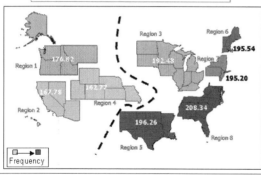

Adding color coding by frequency and displaying data on a geographic reference allows a pattern to emerge

Looking for trends is part of data analysis. If you look at your data and see something seriously harming your bottom line or an opportunity that needs to be grabbed immediately—you take action. Trends are more subtle than data points you jump on right away. Trends are slight directional changes over time or correlations among different data categories collected simultaneously. Finding trends and making a proactive response allows you to avoid situations that require emergency, all-out action.

Patterns of change

What do customers want or need in the future?

What derivative problems or unintended consequences will need a solution?

Is the change a trend or a fad?

Is the trend a function of changes in technology, the economy, environment, or society?

Minimize uncertainty

Real-time monitoring

Optimize complex processes

Data-Driven Trend Analysis

One approach to trend analysis is statistical. By applying algorithms to data, you can see if your performance reflects normal process variation or if there is a real trend in the direction of the data. In the example above, you want to know if last month's 930 errors were typical or higher than normal. By looking at your average error rates, you see that 930 errors is pretty close to average, within one, standard deviation of the mean—certainly not elevated enough to cause you to do something different.

If you want to practice continual improvement by lowering your errors per month, you might choose to compare each future month against your benchmark, or you can create a trend line and measure its slope over time to see if the direction is the desired one, even if the value differences are not statistically significant. Finally, you can plot just the changes in the average or mean. Any of these techniques will give you a window into trends in your organization's performance.

Intuitive Trend Analysis

Another approach to trend analysis is intuitive. Instead of using numeric data, intuitive trend analysis relies on knowledge gained on the job or in the world. Intuitive trend analysis is a *sense* of what is normal or a *feeling* that something is unusual. Intuitive trend analysis shouldn't be shunned because it seems less scientific than a data-driven approach. Business leaders, famous investors, inventors, researchers, and other professionals often rely on intuition-based trend analysis.

Daniel Isenberg, senior lecturer of business administration at the Harvard Business School in the Entrepreneurial Management Unit, tells us from his research on intuition[xxix] that senior managers and leaders use intuition to identify when a problem exists, to synthesize isolated bits of data and experience into an integrated picture—sometimes called an "aha" moment, as a check on the output of "rational" or data-driven analysis and when the need to move quickly forestalls formal data collection and analysis. Intuitive identification of a trend can also provide the impetus to collect confirming data.

In a classic case of intuitive trend analysis, Winn Schwartau, author of *Information Warfare,* relates a story about how just prior to the first Gulf War, a foreign government could have deduced an imminent military action: "We knew the night before the Gulf War because of all the pizza orders heading to the Pentagon" Schwartau deduced, using the number of people working late based on cars in the Pentagon parking lot and the number of delivered pizzas as indicators, something unusual was going on.

115

Fp

Fix problems don't blame

When something is going wrong with a project or a product, it is tempting to find out who is at fault and blame them. There is even a holiday (the first Friday the 13th of the year) called Blame-Someone-Else Day.

As you grew older and more mature, you learned that blaming someone did not change the outcome or improve future performance, and the person who was singled out for blame was not always friendly or helpful afterward. Now, as a leader and a manager, it may still be tempting on occasion to affix blame when there is a problem, but just as in childhood, fixing blame does not improve the situation. If anything, spending time looking for someone to blame will delay solving the problem or fixing the situation. Blaming is passive, detrimental, and discouraging. It is immature. Attaching blame to someone or something external is the opposite of taking responsibility.

The only way to change reality is to fix the problem. After you have done what you can and are back on track for success, then perhaps there may be some merit to understanding what happened. But even here, you are not seeking to blame someone. Rather, you want to know if there is a systemic reason for a bad outcome—a reason that can be addressed so there are no identical, future problems.

There is a long-term benefit to fixing problems instead of blaming—you model for your employees the importance of reaching your goals, even in adversity, you show them that when mistakes happen, they must be addressed, and you do not encourage them to find someone to blame themselves.

EXERCISES

Exercise 1
Finding the Vital Few

Make a list and zero in

Key indicators are those data points or sets that provide the most useful information with the least amount of time required for collection and analysis. For this exercise, pick a large project or function, brainstorm all the indicators or status, progress, or problems you can think of, then rank the list and select only the top three.

Type of data	When to collect	How will you use the data?

For each selected piece of data, why is it one of the vital few?

1. _____
2. _____
3. _____

Exercise 2
Trend Analysis

Getting Ideas

Select a major, future event in the news – global warming, health care costs, retiring boomers – and choose an event that represents a potential major change for your organization.

How could this event or condition effect your organization?

How will you know?

What information should you collect?

Chapter 16: Align with Management Levers

Introduction: Leadership is inspiring others to do something different or something better. Management is about pulling levers to make something happen. As a manager, you have several, solid levers available to you to help create a motivated and capable workforce, but you need to use these levers wisely by making sure they are aligned with each other to maximize your results. Your journey begins with deciding what you want and need from your employees. Next, communicate those expectations to employees and motivate them while letting them play to their strengths to meet those expectations. Finally, provide tools and training to ensure success, and reward them when they accomplish their goals and meet the organization's needs.

What you will learn in this chapter:

Why reorganization should not be your first or even second choice to solve a problem
- What questions should you ask yourself before reorganizing
- When is reorganization a good choice

The importance of consistent commitment to staff development
- Types of staff development activities
- Guidelines on staff development

The importance of using measurement
- Why measurement is important to you and the organization
- The use of measurement in managing staff performance

Rewards and reinforcement
- Guidelines for giving rewards to employees
- Types of rewards that work

Conversation isn't just talking
- The value of two-way conversations
- Characteristics of useful conversation

Nothing is more important than selecting the right staff
- What is an effective process for identifying good potential employees
- Interview strategies

8

Ar

Try to avoid reorganization

Reorganization often involves shuffling the deck and expecting different cards to appear. The problem is, the same cards seem to keep showing up. There are a few valid reasons to reorganize, but they do *not* include moving out a problem manager, not knowing what else to do, collaborating or coordinating failure between organization components, or making changes simply because its been two years since the last reorganization.

Why be cautious about playing the reorganization card? Because it can negatively impact organizational performance for months, if not years. It can be disruptive to employees' working lives and cause unnecessary anxiety as people jockey for position and rebuild those informal relationships that help get things done. Remember, over time, all solutions reveal their own problems.

Valid reasons to partially reorganize may include the loss of a major business component or funding source, a production of a new product, a new strategic initiative, a new acquisition, or a merger with another organization.

Before You Reorganize, Ask Yourself:

- Why do I want to reorganize? What's the problem I want to solve?
- What can the new organization do that the old organization can't do as well?
- What other options can we try to solve the problem before reorganization? Remember, a reorganization is disruptive, costly, and will take at least a year to recover from.
- What will be the impact on productivity and employee morale of the reorganization? How will that impact translate into costs?
- If reorganization solves a problem, have you considered other, less-disruptive ways to do it?
- Have you completed a cost/benefit analysis of the reorganization?
- How will you know if the reorganization is accomplishing its goals? What are the measures for success?

Employees want to grow professionally, learn new skills, and have opportunities to improve themselves. You want your staff to continually improve their job performance and take on additional responsibilities. You and your employees can reach these objectives through organized and supported staff development. Great managers know how to move an employee along a career path through orchestrated learning experiences — the key word being *orchestrated*.

The way you structure training depends, to some extent, on the size of your organization. Large organizations usually have staff development and training departments that setup and oversee training by position and tasks. In smaller organizations, training may be completed by outside consultants or vendors.

The real development challenge for a manager is unstructured training, which is accomplished through job assignments, mentoring, and informal training — learning to do a job by doing the job with supportive guidance.

As a manager and leader, you have a significant responsibility to grow your workforce via task assignments and delegation of responsibility. You need to spend a lot of your time on this to do it well. Here are some guidelines:

Guidelines on Developing Your Staff

- Know how you will evaluate task performance, and share that with your employees.
- Select new tasks that stretch employees' skills and responsibilities.
- Have high, but realistic, expectations.
- Do *not* add new tasks or responsibility solely to correct weaknesses — this is setting yourself up for failure. Whenever possible, let employees play to their strengths.
- Encourage your staff to suggest areas and jobs they would like to learn more about, and look for opportunities to give them that experience.
- Share tips and stories from your own experience and help others learn through listening and observation.
- Encourage your other managers to make opportunities for their employees' growth and to share their lessons learned.
- Ask someone who does a job very well to discuss or present "what I wish I'd known before … "

34

M

Measure

Measurement is more than scoring. Measurement shows how well you are meeting objectives, gives indicators of the need for change, and helps you explain and persuade. High-level performance measures should align with the mission and vision of the organization. For day-to-day operations, performance measures should be tied to goals and objectives.

Establishing performance measures in the beginning helps you assess your status and direct actions. Get a consensus among the stakeholders on what the correct performance measures are, and then periodically measure performance against those parameters.

When you hire someone or change employee assignments, tell them how their performance will be measured. Knowing how well they are doing a job helps employees focus and prioritize their efforts.

Tip: Remember, keep all these levers aligned or they can work against one another. Using the previous element (Development), you might train employees on new practices while measurements hold them accountable for the old. Now, instead of putting the two elements together for even more leverage, they cancel each other out!

Measurement allows you to compare actual performance against plans and objectives. Measurement tells you when you are succeeding and when you need to change course. It also helps you sell ideas to stakeholders — either explaining status and plans or persuading them to support a new idea or objective. Using performance measures that specify how long, how much, and how well may tip a decision your way.

52

Rw

Reward

Rewarding people for a job well done is the right thing to do, but it also serves many other organizational purposes. For the person being rewarded, a reward makes them feel good, they understand that you recognize their efforts, and they are very likely to perform even better for the organization. Others who see that someone is rewarded for their efforts learn which behaviors are rewarded and often strive to do better as well.

Although annual salary increments and bonuses are rewarding, they are often very distant in time from the actions that are being rewarded and can lose some of their punch in reinforcing exceptional behaviors. However, if everyone receives an annual increment, it becomes expected and is not seen as a reward.

Many types of rewards can be used. A reward for exceptional performance should be made as close in time to the events as possible. There are high-value rewards, such as a promotion or a raise in salary, but not all reward systems require money. Recognition in the form of praise, a letter of commendation, or a "well done," goes a long way toward telling an employee his work is valued and appreciated.

Tip: Informal rewards, like a pat on the back, often have more impact than formal rewards.

Here are some characteristics on the effective use of rewards:

Guidelines on Using Rewards

- Make it clear what actions are being rewarded and make the reward timely.
- Make sure you have a formal performance reward program, and the evaluation criteria are fully understood and within the control of the person being rewarded.
- Use spontaneous rewards frequently, especially for group efforts — give an afternoon off, host a picnic in the parking lot, provide tickets to a local sporting event or movie theater, etc.
- Be sure the rewards are based on behaviors or actions of the individual.
- Use semiformal communication tools, like the corporate intranet, newsletter, or memos, to recognize someone's achievements.
- Give the reward personally, and tell the person why he or she is being rewarded.
- Invite the successful employee to have lunch or coffee with you.
- Team awards should be based on team performance. You may choose to have separate reward programs for individual and team accomplishments.
- A handwritten note with praise from you can be remarkably motivating.

84

Tw

Open two-way conversations

Listen

Involve

Encourage

Give Feedback

Get Feedback

Although "open two-way conversations" may sound like a simple instruction, it is a complex and challenging concept that requires a strong foundation of trust between management and employees. Two-way conversation means both parties talk and both parties listen. Conversation requires understanding, otherwise it is just noise. The requirements for effective two-way communication include:

- **Share Information** — both parties need to know all the facts, objectives, and constraints.
- **Respect Everyone** — in the conversation, you must believe and act without bias for age, sex, education level, or position of the other participants.
- **Trust** — a shared belief that you can depend on each other to achieve a common purpose.
- **Honesty** — in all things is needed.
- **Completeness** — not selective representation of facts.
- **No retribution** — even if you do not like what you hear.
- **Openness** — if you communicate either orally or through your body language that you have already made up your mind, there can be no honest, two-way communication.
- **Reciprocity** — the give-and-take between two or more people. This give-and-take should be open-ended and not controlled by any single participant.
- **Active listening** — paraphrase what you hear back to the speaker.
- **Commitment** — if you agree to do something, do it; or explain why you can't.
- **Communicate Status** — if a topic requires collecting more information or gaining someone else's input, let the initiator know the status periodically and in a timely fashion.
- **Inform** — participants about decisions.

Organizations benefit greatly from effective, two-way communication. First, informed and participating employees are more willing to sign on to projects with demanding and changing requirements. Second, to paraphrase a cliché from the 1960s, if employees are part of the solution, they are less likely to be part of a problem. Third, your employees have a lot to tell you that can positively impact the effectiveness of your decisions — you need to listen to them.

Staffing is one of the most challenging and important tasks managers face. **Read the Mega-Tip below!** Without the right people, no amount of money can make an organization succeed. The wrong person can have destructive impact on the entire organization. The goals of staffing are three-fold, find someone who: **can** do the job, **wants** to do the job, and **will do** the job. You reach the staffing goals by identifying potential employees, interviewing them, hiring them and preparing them to be contributors to the organization through orientation and training.

"If you pick the right people and give them the opportunity to spread their wings—and put compensation as a carrier behind it—you almost don't have to manage them."[xxx]
—Jack Welch

To select the right talent first, you must clearly define the tasks or role of the position. What do you want the person to do for your organization and how you will measure their success? Take some time to brainstorm with your team the skills and experience necessary to accomplish the job – it's always an excellent idea to get input from other staff about expectations because when someone is already doing a similar job, they understand what the new person needs to do. Write down the job tasks, skills required, and performance measures to be used. The exercise of writing this information down will sharpen solicitation of applicants, your interviewing, and your selection.

"Surround yourself with the best people you can find, delegate authority, and don't interfere as long as the policy you've decided upon is being carried out."[xxxi]
—Ronald Reagan

MEGA TIP: 1) Select an individual's traits and not simply skills and experience. For example, if you are selecting someone for a supervisory slot, traits like optimism, concern for others, and drive are far better predictors of success than having three years of past experience supervising. 2) Psychologists say everyone thinks their judgment is better than the next person's. Be aware of this when panels make selections and always use professional assessors or validated tools to boost predictability. When it comes to selection, the difference between your common sense and scientific selection approaches are tremendous.

Advanced Tip: Using non-scientifically validated questioning (unstructured interviews) can get you better than random selection results – a validity coefficient of .25 to .3. Using scientifically proven systems like structured interviews or computer interactive talent assessments can boost that to .5 or higher. That margin of difference is huge and means you won't be suffering from bad choices nearly as often. If the management chain in your organization hasn't improved over the last five or ten years, it's because you are still using the same old unscientific selection interview process.

When you find a promising candidate, respond quickly to their application. Before scheduling a face-to-face interview, screen the candidate on the phone. You don't want to waste your time on someone who, with a little investigation, can be ruled out as a candidate.

Interviews must be two way communications. You want to provide the applicant with information about the job expectations and about the company. You should describe what it is like to work at your company, how you evaluate performance, and the career path from the position for which he or she is applying. You are also trying to find out if the applicant meets your three criteria and will **fit** into the team. The answers to these questions are sometimes subjective and require judgment. Have applicants interview with several people including the hiring supervisor, someone in a similar job, a human resource representative, and a senior manager so you get various perspectives.

Clearly listen to the answers to see that the applicant understands the job requirements and is willing to make a commitment to the project and the organization. Consider the questions the applicant asks you. Are they curious about the company's future? Or, are they more concerned about benefits and working conditions? Does the applicant demonstrate knowledge about your company based on research done before the interview?

Keep in mind that a candidate may have all the needed skills and attitudes, but still not fit the project or the organization. Remember, it's their traits that are critical because you can always train skills. Ask yourself if this person can work effectively in your environment and if you, personally, would like to work with them. Below are a few guidelines to facilitate effective staffing.

Guidelines to Find and Hire the Right Talent for your Organization

- Working with appropriate staff, define the tasks to be done and how performance will be measured. What are the traits (strengths) you want in an ideal candidate? Use this description to solicit candidates and structure the interview topics.
- Let existing employees know when you are look for candidates. Your staff knows the job and the organization. They can be salespeople for you and good screeners.
- In addition to talking about the job, include job expectations such as required travel, overtime, and expected code of conduct.
- Have some of your the best employees interview the candidate.
- Gain consensus on your selection. Understand what your interviewers liked or did not like about the candidate. Trust their gut instincts even if they cannot articulate what did not feel quite right to them or why they really liked someone.

- Don't expect perfection. Hire the best overall fit for your organization's future. Hire someone who is able to do most of what needs to be done, but also shows the willingness and ability to learn more.
- Staffing does not end with the decision to hire or the acceptance by the candidate. You need to bring the new hire up to speed through orientation, mentoring, and feedback throughout the critical first six months.
- DO NOT compromise your standards. The price you pay for hiring the wrong person is too high.
- Use scientific selection tools to assist since this is the most important decision a manager can make. Employ outside professionals to help with this. Let their professional assessments supplement your common sense. This vastly increases your probability of making a good decision.

EXERCISES

Exercise 1
Rewards

Rewarding employees for a job well done or service beyond expectations is important, challenging, and fun.

Make a list of five nonmonetary rewards you can give to your employees:

1. _____
2. _____
3. _____
4. _____
5. _____

Exercise 2
Selecting the Right Talent

You are going to hire a new project manager. The job requires someone who can work across the organization and is especially skilled at motivating employees because the deadlines for this project are very tight.

Q&A

What questions would you ask?	What answers would you like to hear?

Chapter 17: Walk Before You Run

Once you know where you want your organization to be and how you want to get there, patience may be difficult to come by. Knowing where you want to go and getting there in a judicious manner requires some small steps and basic skill acquisition first. You need to walk before you can run.

In this chapter, we look at some of the foundational basics to have in place before you try to get too tricky with things like Six Sigma or Matrix Management. This chapter provides steps to take before jumping in and making sweeping changes.

Core skill areas of leaders and managers
- Traits that make a good leader
- Essential, basic, management operating principles

The importance of interpersonal skills
- Working through others to reach goals
- Undesirable behaviors that impede personal interactions

How basic metrics help you understand your organization
- Characteristics of effective metrics
- Types of metrics

Decentralized decision making supports effectiveness and efficiency
- The benefits of decentralized decision making
- Understanding how decisions are made in your organization

Why your organization should value learning
- Learning is an adaptive, change process
- Data you need to direct organizational learning

What the Baldrige Award means
- How an organization is recognized by the NIST's Baldrige Award
- Who are Baldrige winners

Bp

Basic management and leadership principles

Management is the process of helping other people reach agreed objectives and accomplish tasks. Management includes planning, organizing, problem solving, staffing, and directing people, money, and resources. Leadership adds strategy and vision to management. Managers execute the mission while leaders inspire people to higher performance levels. Neither leadership nor management is governed by scientific certainties, but solid principles can help you from flying-by-the-seat-of-your-pants and making beginners' mistakes.

Principles of good management and leadership include communication, delegation, enabling, fact-based decision making, and fair recognition supported by a foundation of beliefs about the right way to treat people.

Communication:
- Provide all the necessary information, frequently
- Ask questions
- Listen actively
- Clarify

Delegation:
- Set objectives and let others determine how to meet them
- Push decision making as low as possible in the organization

Enabling:
- Train and develop employees
- Remove barriers
- Share knowledge

Fact-based decision making:
- Collect metrics
- Do not let emotions overcome facts

Fair recognition:
- Base recognition on facts
- Accept and expect accountability
- Reward
- Be timely

Leadership principles are an attitude displayed through daily behaviors. They describe the basic concepts of how an organization and a leader should act toward others.

Interpersonal skills, sometimes called social skills, are those behaviors that facilitate interactions with other people. These core skills are usually developed by the early twenties but can be polished at any age with awareness, practice, and feedback. Interpersonal skills determine to a great extent how successfully you manage, negotiate, influence, and lead.

One great leader at the CIA says, "I make sure there are no barriers between me and the other person, so I get up from behind my desk and sit directly across from them. That way I can focus on what they are saying." On the other hand, one can learn from examples of poor interpersonal skills that bad bosses sometimes display:

Listen

Eye contact

Behaviors that Harm the Effectiveness of Your Interpersonal Interactions

Smile

- Thinking everything can be resolved with logical analysis
- Believing anyone who does not agree with you is stupid
- Believing that facts should be sufficient to motivate people
- Actively running away from conflict, power struggles, and divided loyalties

Accept

- Believing that other people should work harder to understand what you are saying
- Not listening to people who do not speak within your frame of reference

Ask questions

- Interrupting
- Rushing peoples' thoughts

Friendly

- Showing impatience
- Asking "gotcha" questions
- Distrusting emotion and intuition in analysis and decision making

Trust

- Believing that problems have one, and only one, correct solution
- Preferring e-mail and texting to a face-to-face meeting
- Believing you should win a debate
- Believing you have to be right

Metrics are numbers used to compare two or more characteristics of an outcome or process. They are measurements taken over time that assess and communicate information about performance.

If metrics overwhelm you, remember, almost all metrics fall into a combination of the following, four categories: quantity, quality, effort, and effect. Don't forget about time, which can be a reliable measure to track productivity or process efficiency. And remember, you own the metrics—they don't own you. Be bold and scrap metrics that don't work for you.

Although some performance-management systems can become complex, basic metrics are simple and straightforward. Basic metrics can be as simple as counting things on your toes and are very powerful aids to planning, decision making, and information sharing.

How We Measure Shoe Size

Have you ever wondered why your shoe size is what it is? Back in simpler times, people measured with what was available:

A shoe that was a hand's breadth long (about four inches) was the smallest, and two hand's breadths was the largest size for children.

Add a third hand's breadth for a man's shoe.

Feet are unforgiving, so you need intermediate sizes. Barley was a prevalent English crop, so British shoemakers used the length of a barley grain to measure size differences—three barleycorns makes an inch.

If you live in France, start with the hands' breadth but go ahead and forget about the barleycorns and use two-thirds of a centimeter for your size differences.

American shoe sizes are one number off from British sizes because they call the smallest size a zero while Americans call it a one.

A basic performance measure is composed of a number and a unit of measure. The number gives us "how much" and the unit tells us "of what." Performance measures are usually tied to a goal or an objective that adds context to the "how-much-of-what" metric. Here are some examples of basic metrics:

- Number of sales per month
- Number of potential customers contacted per week
- Hours of overtime worked per employee
- Monthly fuel costs
- Time required to process customer orders

Remember, using visual displays (element 51) can greatly facilitate comparison between measures and rapid understanding of current status.

Finally, to avoid having too many metrics, weed them out by asking the following questions:

- Are the metrics good indicators of the performance in which you are interested?
- Are the metrics clear and unequivocal?
- Are the metrics easy to collect?
- Will knowing the answer provided by the metrics help make a future decision or understand a current status?
- Are the number and complexity of the metrics reasonable?
- Are the metrics tracked regularly?
- What is the source of the data?
- Does everyone involved understand and agree with the metrics being collected?

53

Dm

Decentralize decision making

Hierarchical, decision-making structures that permit only senior managers to approve actions and expenditures can be a tremendous time sink, making your organization less agile and responsive. Push authority for management actions as far down into the organization as possible. "But won't that create chaos?" you ask. No, not if you balance the delegation with accountability; just make sure subordinates understand outcomes, and use simple outcome metrics described in the previous element.

This is how you benefit: Employees are the grease in the gears of your organization if they perceive they have the right to make local improvements without having to say, "Mother may I?" When employees feel free to make decisions appropriate for their level, you engage all the brains in the organization and not just the ones at the top—that's a huge, competitive advantage. If employees think they aren't supposed to think, they convert from the grease to the sand in your organizational gears.

When employee (and subordinate manager) brain's are engaged, problems are addressed sooner and at a lower cost. Without engaging lower-level brains, problems fester, improvements don't occur, and organizations ossify.

Think of low-level problems as little isotopes flitting around the bottom of your organization. When employees don't sweep them away on a daily basis, they begin to join together into compounds, and suddenly a larger, more complex problem erupts at your level

> **Interesting study[xxxii]:** Michael Williamson at the University of Texas Austin found that
>
> "Experimental results demonstrate that employees with a joint role in choosing firm activities evaluated the decision-making environment of the firm to be fairer which led them to derive greater enjoyment from their work environment which ultimately led them to contribute a greater amount to the firm."
>
> Despite the fact that they contributed more to the firm, the employees didn't expect higher rewards. That's not bad is it? Happier employees, more trust, higher employee contribution—and it's all free for the asking.

If it's not a decision that is crucial to organizational survival or something that must be decided upon this minute, reach down for ideas and recommendations. See if you can decentralize decisions in budgeting, budget allocation, staffing, scheduling, reimbursements, rewards, customer service, and internal process improvement. .If you choose not to take subordinates' advice, signal back why—otherwise it's insulting.

Look what you gain with decentralized decision making:

How Decentralized Decision Making Improves Your Organization

- Empowerment—empowered employees are more loyal to the organization, more creative in solving problems, and more committed to assuring successful outcomes.
- Agility—when decision and actions are closer to the problem, the organization can act more quickly to solve them.
- Better decisions—grassroots staff understand the problems and potential solutions better than those individuals who are far removed from the action.
- Customer satisfaction—if those directly involved with customers and clients have the authority to act, then clients and customers feel happier and better served.
- Flexibility—Planning, problem solving, production, and service can be more flexible and individualized within a decentralized decision management system.
- Creativity—The experience and creativity of many people are focused on solving local business challenges. Using effective knowledge sharing (elements 50 and 106), the organization can tap this broad expertise and creativity for organizational improvement.

85

Lo

Learning organization

Understand trends

Stay in touch with customers needs

Be willing to adapt

Several elements presented the advantages of honing and enhancing your skill set (see elements 27, 38, 45, 77, and 109) through continual learning, but did you know that organizations can learn too? Organizations have a memory and can learn new ways of doing things. This is critical in a dynamic, global, and competitive environment.

One of the early proponents of organizational learning was Peter Senge, an MIT professor and author of *The Fifth Discipline*. Senge defines a "learning organization" as one "in which you cannot *not* learn because learning is so insinuated into the fabric of life." He believes that a learning organization has a philosophy that anticipates, reacts and responds to change—it learns. He concludes: "The rate at which organizations learn may become the only sustainable source of competitive advantage."

There are some other interesting perspectives on organizational learning that come from the community of scientists studying complex adaptive systems (CAS), of which organizations are examples. CASs

Be introspective about the organizational impact of your processes and procedures

change and learn from experience. Although the roots of CAS come from the biological sciences, when applied to business, they point us to the importance of expectations and feedback.

The lesson from CAS is that a leader must model and encourage an organization toward the view that learning is essential to survival. Otherwise, organizations develop business blind spots, like Westinghouse, Hoffman-La Roche, Sears, Digital, Tandy, and Encyclopedia Britannica did in the past. Or, for example, when bankrupt Schwinn Bicycles didn't see the mountain bike trend coming, Kodak missed digital cameras for many years, and GM missed lean production. You don't want your organization to be part of that historical list.

Case study: The U.S. Army learned this lesson with its Zero Defects effort. Mistakes were a black mark. Junior officers, sergeants, and the troops quickly recognized it was better to do nothing than risk making an error. The lesson was that assigning blame often produces fear and curtails innovation.

Today, the army debriefs everyone after training or combat. These sessions are blameless—it's the only time an enlisted soldier can openly criticize an officer. The results get sent to the Center for Army Lessons Learned[xxxiii] in Fort Leavenworth and are quickly used to produce new doctrine and policy.

117

BI

(win) Baldrige Award

"The greatest leader I ever knew was Secretary of Commerce, Malcolm Baldrige. Baldrige was kind, humble, concerned about his employees, and a man of phenomenal judgment and common sense. July 25, 1987 was the day the U.S. Department of Commerce cried when Baldrige died in a tragic rodeo accident in California. Two decades later my wife, Pat, returned from a meeting with Commerce employees to tell me,

Cadillac

Texas Instruments

Robert Wood Johnson Hospital

U. S. Army Armament Research

Ritz-Carlton

Granite Rock Company

Branch-Smith Printing

Dana Corporation

Pearl River School District

*Los Alamos National Bank*

*Zytec Corporation*

*Marlow Industries*

*Jenks Public Schools*

'They're still talking about Mac Baldrige!' Truly great leaders have that kind of lasting impact."

A commitment to quality improvement is the best way to stay in business and to prosper. Quality and attending to your customers really does matter! This was even recognized by the U.S. Congress. In 1988, Congress established the Malcolm Baldrige National Quality Award — America's highest honor for performance excellence — to promote quality awareness. The award categories, which include manufacturing, service, small business, education, and health care, were expanded in October 2004 to include nonprofit organizations.

The core values of the Baldrige review include

- Visionary leadership
- Customer-driven excellence
- Organizational and personal learning
- Valuing employees and partners
- Agility
- Focusing on the future
- Managing for innovation
- Managing by fact
- Social responsibility
- Focusing on results and creating value
- Systems perspective

Winning a Baldrige Award requires detailed, internal review and site visits from specialists who evaluate processes, procedures, and outcomes in the following areas:

- **Leadership** — how senior executives guide the organization and how the organization addresses its responsibilities to the public and practices good citizenship.
- **Strategic planning** — how the organization sets strategic directions and how it determines key action plans.
- **Customer and market focus** — how the organization determines requirements and expectations of customers and markets; builds relationships with customers; and acquires, satisfies, and retains customers.
- **Measurement, analysis, and knowledge management** — the management, effective use, analysis, and improvement of data and information to support key organization processes and the organization's performance-management system.

City of Coral Springs

Mercy Health System

MESA Products

- **Workforce focus** — how the organization enables its workforce to develop its full potential and how the workforce is aligned with the organization's objectives.
- **Process management** — how key production/delivery and support processes are designed, managed, and improved.
- **Results in the organization's performance and improvement in its key business areas** — customer satisfaction, financial and marketplace performance, human resources, supplier and partner performance, operational performance, and governance and social responsibility. The category also examines how the organization performs relative to competitors.

EXERCISES

Exercise 1
Decentralized Decision Making

Who has the authority?

*Here are four organization situations.
For each, think about who has the
authority to change the standard
operating process or procedure on the
spot. Is this the best management level
for these decisions? Can the authority
be pushed lower in the organization?*

1. A salesman has taken an excellent, potential client out to lunch. The client wants to split his order over two deliveries (against efficiency procedures). Can the salesman make an agreement for special processing?

2. A client needs special assistance getting to his appointment. Can the caseworker use petty cash funds to pay for a taxi (not in current policy)?

3. A software vendor is offering one of your departments the opportunity to test out new software to promote efficiency in handling financials. Can the department manager accept the offer?

4. A regular customer is short of cash to pay for his small purchase. Can the salesman or manager agree to let him have the product and pay later?

Exercise 2
Learning Organizations

*What have you done in the last year
that you consider supportive of
organizational learning? What else
can you do this year?*

What did you do this year?

1. _____

2. _____

3. _____

What can you do next year?

1. _____

2. _____

3. _____

Chapter 18: Know Your Organization

You have reached a milestone. Chapter 18, Knowing Your Organization, is a crucial step in becoming a great manager, just as its partner at the other end of the chart—chapter 1, Know Yourself—is crucial to becoming a great leader. These bookends hold together the leadership elements on the left side of the chart and the management elements on the right. However, knowing your organization is tougher than it sounds because like high-energy particles, many of these elements are invisible to the eye.

At birth, organizations reflect the vision and character of their founders but as they mature, collective behaviors, processes and procedures, and the management chain define the organizational values. These values may have good and bad sides to them, and the negative parts, like barnacles, build up on the organization. It's good from time to time to stop cruising blithely forward and take stock of these by using the following elements to check up on organizational health.

What you will learn in this chapter:

Remembering your vision
- Live your organization's vision
- Teach and discuss your organization's vision

Maintaining realistic assessment of strengths and weaknesses
- How to learn about your organization's strengths and weaknesses
- Which strengths and weaknesses make a difference in your organization's future

Culture is everywhere
- Learn about your organization's culture
- Changing culture when it no longer works to your advantage

Be on the lookout for opportunities and threats
- Be aware of threats from unexpected directions
- Seek opportunities from your customers

The importance of understanding your employees as individuals
- What do employee want
- What you must do to improve your understanding of the employees in your organization

Understanding the impact of processes and procedures on your employees

Assessing how your management chain helps or hinders meeting your goals

2	
	F
	Know heading (vision and strategy)

In achieving element 2, Know heading (vision and strategy), define where you want your organization to be in the future. Your vision represents your belief about how your organization fits within the greater business environment and the marketplace. What do you want to *become*? This element implies direction and movement and not simply a state of being.

In the heat of everyday problem solving, vision can get lost. As an organization leader, it is your job to remind and refresh the corporate memory about the organization's vision. Begin with yourself. As you prepare your state-of-the-organization reports or your orientation to new employees, be sure to reference your vision and your directional heading; cite examples and realistic goals or steps along the path. Live your vision through your actions.

To keep everyone mindful of the organization's vision, make sure that strategic plans and metrics capture information that reflects on progress in realizing the organization's vision. Use compliance with your vision when selecting alternative actions. Reward employees whose actions exemplify the vision and help move the organization forward.

Here are some succinct vision statements that succeeded in driving organizational behavior:

- **Option One Mortgage**: be widely recognized as the premier provider of innovative financial products and services.
- **John F. Kennedy:** land a man on the moon and safely return him to earth by the end of this decade.
- **Northrop Grumman:** become the premier supplier of reliable, high-quality, complex, military-defense systems and commercial, aerospace products.
- **General Electric:** become the most competitive enterprise in the world by being number one or number two in market share in every sector.

Important: It's far better to have a vision than to have a vision statement. Organizations score negative points for posting vision statements on the wall that remain unpracticed day to day.

Sw

Know strengths and weaknesses

Reasons for your successes

Characteristics of your failures

Branding

Cash cows

Organizational Dogs

Intellectual capital

Knowing your organizational strengths and weaknesses gives you a tremendous competitive advantage, while not knowing them hands an advantage to competitors and detractors. Professional sports teams draft players to shore up their weaknesses and plan game strategies that magnify their strengths. They study game footage, they talk to players, and they listen to knowledgeable commentators because they don't want to be deceived by wishful thinking. They want to win.

It's crucial to know strengths as well. You can use your strengths to increase market share, win contracts, and maintain a position of leadership in your industry. You can assess your strengths in terms of people, products, customer loyalty, responsiveness, agility, creativity or problem solving — there are many ways to slice this pie.

Tip: When you understand real strengths, you can advertise your organization with believable facts, not hype.

Another important part of knowing your strengths is to objectively understand the strengths of individual employees. A good manager knows that not all employees work the same way. For the organization to be successful, they put employees in jobs that allow them to use their strengths. Practice your skills at spotting the unique strengths in each employee, and then capitalize on them.

A & C Black Publishers Ltd provides an informative article called "Analyzing Your Business's Strengths, Weaknesses, Opportunities, and Threats" or SWOT. The essence of the SWOT analysis is to discover what you do well, how you could improve, whether you are making the most of the opportunities around you, and whether there are any changes in your market, such as technological developments or shifting environmental factors that may require corresponding changes in your business. The article provides good suggestions on how to carry out your own SWOT analysis.

A corporation or organization's culture is most easily defined as, "the way we do things here." Cultures don't change quickly but they can evolve. As generations of new managers and employees interpret the culture and place their own spin on it, the culture slowly changes.

As a manager and leader, you should periodically take a fix on your corporate culture. The further removed you are from day-to-day operations (i.e., the higher you are in the hierarchy), the more important it is for you to know the current culture. Some areas that are frequently considered part of the corporate culture include core values, practiced beliefs (as opposed to those posted on the wall), corporate ethics, and actual behaviors. Glance over some of the following questions to examine your corporate culture:

- Do employees feel free to take risks?
- How are decisions made, and how are those decisions communicated to staff?
- Does the environment feel friendly or cutthroat and highly competitive where only one person can win?
- How do the employees interact with customers?
- Is there natural collaboration between units?
- Is there a formal or informal dress code?
- Are the offices and cubicles individually decorated, or do they all have a corporate "look and feel"?
- Does employee training freely discuss corporate values?
- How do you demonstrate the value you place on employees? Are there onsite perks, such as break rooms, workout facilities, or daycare? Do you have flextime options? Do employees have a career path?
- How much time outside the office do your employees spend with co-workers?

We all think we know our organizational culture, but to sharpen your understanding, examine how the culture is being implemented from the viewpoint of those deeper in the organization. Have groups of employees circle the top five organizational values off the list of organizational values on www.mikemears.biz. Collect these to see what employees think—that's probably the best measure of your culture.

Whether your organization is a profit or nonprofit service provider, you have opportunities for growth, and there are threats in the marketplace that can derail your best strategies. It is essential to actively monitor both. You need to know what opportunities are out there, and you need to know about threats.

By following the Elements of Leadership and Management, you've given yourself the tools you need to understand opportunities and threats through learning, data collection, and direct interaction with your employees and your customers. In a sense, that is the easy part—getting the information.

Caution! Do not allow your subordinates to tell you what they think you want to hear. It may feel good, but it can lead to blindsiding or catastrophic failure.

To recognize and act on opportunities and threats, you need to do something that may be much more difficult—you have to be brutally honest with yourself and your organization. Wishful thinking, misdirected attention, plausible deniability, or selective acceptance are detrimental to understanding opportunities and threats.

So how do you identify and assess opportunities? Begin with the knowledge you have accumulated about your industry, products, customer's concerns, and staff ideas. There is a large collection of potential opportunities contained in that knowledge. You turn these potential opportunities into real opportunities by analysis of costs and benefits followed by action. You can spot opportunities by using employee brainstorming, structured analysis, and some out-of-the-box thinking.

The United Kingdom's Chartered Institute of Marketing offers this breakdown for thinking about business growth opportunities.

	Existing	New
Existing	Grow through selling more current products to existing customers	Grow through adding new products or services or modifying existing products or services
New	Grow through selling existing products or services to new customers and markets	Grow through diversification of products and services within the same or similar industry

157

Disruptive technologies

Digital audio players virtually replaced CD players

Telephones replaced telegraphs

3 1/2" diskettes replaced 5 1/4" diskettes, and they were replaced by flash drives and CD disks

Desktop-publishing software almost completely replaced outsourcing to traditional printing companies

Unforeseen threats can hurt your business by impacting profits and even survival. These threats often don't come from your current batch of competitors. Watch out for threats that come from an unexpected direction, including disruptive technologies.

For example, you need to know if a company currently operating in a different field decides to make a run at your market share, so watch for patent applications, hints in industry newsletters, and listen judiciously to gossip. Being mindful of your vulnerabilities, read between the lines, and think like your potential competitor. When you get feedback that your shipments are late or your clients are complaining about reliability, recognize those points of vulnerability and fix them before someone else takes advantage.

Another source of threats is called disruptive technologies or disruptive innovations. According to Harvard Business School's Clayton Christenson, "A disruptive technology or disruptive innovation[xxxiv] is a technological innovation, product, or service that eventually overturns the existing dominant technology or status quo product in the market". These are tricky to see because they may target a portion of the marketplace that you do not serve, and they are frequently more costly or less capable than existing products or services when they first hit the market. It takes vision and analysis to see the threat the innovation could become.

Watch out for disruptive innovations that may encroach into your territory. Plan ahead for counterattacks or preemptive strikes, and don't miss an opportunity to use a disruptive technology to your organization's benefit.

54

Pe

Understand the people

Listen

Ask

Reflect

Get feedback

Give feedback

Study

Read

Before your employees, staff, managers, customers, or vendors took up their organizational roles, they were actually *people*. Sometimes we forget that, but understanding the needs and motivations of people is key to being a better leader and manager. At an individual level, people are different, so it is also important to understand individual strengths and what makes each individual a unique contributor to the organization.

All of us want to be treated with dignity, have our work valued and rewarded, have security and safety, and have some fun along the way. Most people also want to do a good job, have a career path, and help their organization prosper. Read and study your organization's employee surveys, and talk informally with people to understand how their work-lives are progressing. It will help you gain an appreciation of the employee's frustrations, pleasures, and pressures.

Because motivators can vary considerably, you should strive to understand what motivates each individual and makes him or her feel good about being part of the organization. Find out what drives an employee by talking with them in informal settings, by collecting information from them as part of their performance reviews, and by having career planning meetings. You can also surmise some of these factors through observation.

The CEO of a small Texas business superbly understood people. Her knowledge of who was getting married, whose parent was ill, who was putting a child through college or taking classes themselves was extraordinary. Everyone in the organization felt cared about and treated as unique. She knew of employees' hobbies and their contributions to their community outside of the office. She knew their children's names and what pets they had. Her knowledge about each employee allowed her to offer rewards and challenges that worked for that individual. The end result was that people wanted to stay and wanted to make the organization successful because it was *personal*.

Tip: If you haven't built trust with your employees, most of the levers, like rewards and metrics, won't work well. Get the "people part" correct first, and then work on the management levers.

Pp

Know processes and procedures

What is good for the goose is good for the gander—so they say. You should know the organization's processes and procedures because

- You follow them
- You need to understand what is being expected of your employees
- You need to identify inefficiencies that point to potential improvements

The purpose of processes and procedures is to automate decisions. Procedures and processes establish and maintain controls for quality, conformance with regulations, and good management practices.

Over time, however, processes and procedures will become outdated. When everyone worked in the same location within a few hundred feet of one another, having a signature cycle that included three or four approval signatures may have made sense and was not overly burdensome to implement. But now that you have multiple locations, requiring the same number of signatures and the need to maintain a paper trail may be inefficient.

Not only should you know the procedures and processes, you should make sure they are reviewed routinely for applicability to your business today. Practice asking "why" to make sure that the process or procedure is the most appropriate way to accomplish your objectives. Most importantly, solicit input from your staff to improve and simplify processes and procedures whenever possible.

Finally, it's a good idea to have a searchable, online set of processes and procedures so staff can find the most current ones when they are making decisions and performing their routine activities.

Tip: When it comes to process efficiency, make sure you improve a process before bringing in the IT folks. When you automate a bad process, it's frozen in time like a fly in amber, and it becomes more difficult to administer and harder to improve.

U

Understand management chain shortcomings

Is your organization run by:

Theory X

Theory Y

or

Nordstrom Rules

The management chain—the decision-making backbone of an organization—was invented forty-five hundred years ago in Sumer. It allowed people to understand the relative ranking of roles and the relationships among departments and units. This management philosophy was later called Theory X by Douglas McGregor in his classic management text: *The Human Side of Enterprise*[38]. At the time, this hierarchy was a leap forward in managing decision making and problem solving and assigning responsibilities because the average worker performed relatively narrow tasks and had little leeway for creativity. With increased automation and competitiveness, research revealed that the hierarchical chain negatively affected agility, responsiveness, information flow, and process improvement. Hierarchies also promoted fiefdoms and turf consciousness.

Recognizing the limitations of rigid hierarchical management chains led to the concept of Theory Y (flat organizations), which was created in the 1960s by Douglas McGregor. Flat organizations removed layers of management and control in favor of self-directed teams. Whereas rules-based, Theory X organizations tend to have highly centralized decision making, Theory Y organizations tend to have decentralized decision making. As McGregor pointed out in his ground-breaking book, *The Human Side of Enterprise*, management's assumption of how to control people sets the entire tone of the enterprise.

The future of management: New employees at Nordstrom department stores are handed a large box containing the employee handbook and told to memorize the rules. When the box is opened, the single sheet of paper inside reads, "Nordstrom Rules: Rule #1: Use your good judgment in all situations. There will be no additional rules." McGregor would have been pleased by Nordstrom's basic belief that employees have brains and can be trusted to use their judgment.

Ask Yourself

- What is the philosophy of your organization's management chain?
- Are there artifacts in the management chain that handicap you and the organization in reaching your goals and solving problems?
- Is there anything about the chain of command that is detrimental to getting good employees and keeping them?
- Is the chain of management properly matched to your product and your industry?

EXERCISES

**Exercise 1
Organizational Strengths and
Weaknesses**

Playing to Your Strengths and Accommodating
Weaknesses

*The strengths of your organization
are those tangible and intangible
factors that give you an edge over the
competition. List five of your
organization's strengths and why that
strength is important. Then make a
second list of weaknesses. For each
weakness, list a strategy to overcome
or accommodate it.*

Strength	Importance
1.	
2.	
3.	
4.	
5.	

Weakness	Strategy to change or accommodate
1.	
2.	
3.	
4.	
5.	

**Exercise 2
Identifying Threats and
Opportunities**

*Using the strengths and weaknesses
from Exercise 1, develop a list of five
threats and five opportunities. Be
specific. How do you know that you
have a threat? How did you find out
about the opportunities?*

*Extra credit: Pick one opportunity
and develop a business plan to take
advantage.*

Threats:

1. _____
2. _____
3. _____
4. _____
5. _____

Opportunities:

1. _____
2. _____
3. _____
4. _____
5. _____

RARE EARTH ELEMENTS

Introduction

The future holds great promise for organizations that know how to use the time, creativity, and skills of their workers to everyone's advantage. People spend more of their waking lives at work than anywhere else. It is not too extreme to say that companies that are exciting places to be, that value their employees, and that help their employees be productive co-participants in the organization's plans and practices will thrive in the future; organizations that do not will wither and perhaps die.

Future organizations must be as adaptable and innovative as possible. That capability—to jump on new opportunities, to quickly squelch ideas that are failing, to identify and respond to customer needs before the customer can even articulate them—means the organization will rely on the observations, creativity, and commitment of its employees. This future is not a top-down management structure with small, powerful groups analyzing, planning, and managing. It is an organization where every employee is encouraged, challenged, coached, and supported to be part of the solution. Identifying and solving problems is the task of every employee, every day.

The past challenges of management were to create economies of scale, to improve efficiency, to ensure standard compliance, to cut costs, and to decrease inventories. In future organizations, there is a greater emphasis on harnessing "collective intelligence," "information sharing," "reliance on data," and "wisdom of crowds." Although these concepts are borrowed from Web 2.0, they reflect accurately how your future organization will behave. The concepts will motivate your employees to be passionate supporters of your organization and to give their creativity and passion, as well as their skills, to the benefit of the organization. What are the trends driving the need for future organizations that are managed differently than those in the twentieth century?

Organizations in the twenty-first century must contend with the impact of globalization—not just outsourcing low-cost production but also competing for services and white-collar professional skills. The speed with which disruptive technologies are introduced is increasing in response to the information sharing facilitated by the Internet and its sister technologies, like collaborative workspaces, real-time voice and document sharing , and instantly shared data collected via computers and cell phones.

How does a future organization cope with these changes and use them to its advantage? The future organization is skilled at motivating its employees. It views knowledge as a commodity to be shared. You as a leader and manager feel responsible for energizing your employees; you compensate them fairly with full appreciation of the reliance the organization has on their knowledge and commitment. You interact directly with each employee through frequent feedback that is both sought and given, and you are knowledgeable about your employees as individuals and people with lives outside of work. You strive to enable employees to do their jobs and believe they will without extended oversight or management help. You share your vision of where your industry or service organization must go, and above all, you are honest with them and with yourself.

Chapter 19: Our Future Organization

Introduction: Create your future organization by applying and using all the elements in the Inspiration, Improvement, and Implementation groups. The elements themselves are the foundation for those very special organizations labeled "the best" or "world class" — basically, what you want your organization to become. If you apply all the elements we've discussed and add this group of Rare Earth Elements reserved for envied and emulated organizations, your future organization will be in the panoply of highest-performing organizations, not to mention being one great place to work.

What you will learn in this chapter:

- Using failure to improve an organization
- Becoming results oriented
- Realizing the organization's mission
- Your role in energizing employees
- Why a healthy management chain is crucial for improvement
- Prerequisites for an empowered organization
- Using data to make better decisions
- Aligning strategic plans
- Knowledge — knowing what you know
- How to become a more agile organization
- Customers as keys to your success and survival
- Using resources wisely
- Ensuring respect for others is demonstrated in your behavior
- Ways to encourage collaboration
- Streamlining processes to improve profits and reduce frustration

56

Rh

Honor honest failure

- *Know when you are failing.*
- *Get the facts*
- *Decide who to tell*
- *Acknowledge and take responsibility for your part.*
- *Have a plan*
- *Learn and move on.*

Failure is not being where you want to be when you planned to be there. Your team could have missed a deadline, a product didn't meet expectations, a new procedure produced undesirable consequences, or a customer switched to a competitor. The key is to quickly admit failure with open and blameless discussions of what happened and why.

What if you make a mistake yourself? Accepting responsibility for a failure doesn't diminish you—it actually builds your personal credibility as a leader and helps build a little incremental, organizational trust.

How managers address failure within an organization significantly defines organizational culture. Not honoring honest failure sends a message to employees that may lead to cover-ups, lying, or organizational stagnation. Ignoring failure, pretending that everything is going according to plan, or looking for a scapegoat reinforces negative aspects that can do you and your organization irreparable harm.

When you accept honest failure, you provide the impetus to improve or fix a situation, and you also accomplish something that will help your organization in the future—you set an example of the expectation of honesty that your employees will emulate.

Tip: To avoid reinforcing a fear-based culture, acknowledge failure in a nonthreatening way.

57

Ro

Is results oriented

When you undertake a new project, manage an existing

Getting caught up in day-to-day demands often overwhelms the central goal of managers and leaders—getting results. Results are what actually happened, not what you wanted to happen. The daily crisis can be highly distracting, so it's important to keep results in mind and to constantly assess where you are in reaching goals. To do that, it is critical to have a timely information stream and meaningful metrics that give you objective data about your desired outcomes.

Government is often accused of being process rather than results focused. In 1993, Congress passed the Government Performance and Results Act[xxxv] to establish strategic planning and performance

one, or change a process or
procedure, always make sure
you identify what you expect
to accomplish and how you
will assess your success.

measurement in federal organizations and federally funded programs. The act provides good guidance for all of us to be results oriented:

- Establish performance goals to define the level of performance to be achieved by a program activity.
- Express such goals in an objective, quantifiable, and measurable form.
- Describe the operational processes, skills, technology, and the human capital, information, or other resources required to meet the performance goals.
- Establish performance indicators to measure or assess the relevant outputs, service levels, and outcomes of each program activity.
- Provide a basis for comparing the actual program results with the established performance goals.
- Describe the means you'll use to verify and validate measured values.

An added benefit: Focusing the workforce on definable results provides clarity and accountability—it lets employees understand why their job is important. When done correctly, employees are able to assess their own performance against strategic organizational goals and see how their behavior is linked to them—that's a powerful motivator.

58

Ro

Is focused on mission and results

Element 58 differs slightly from element 57 because it reminds you not to lose sight of the organization's mission while striving for results. You don't want to sacrifice where you want to be in the long term for short-term outcomes. It's important to establish a balance between the two. Ideally, short-term plans and interim results are aligned with a larger vision of where the organization is headed and, of course, the organization's mission.

Think of your organization's mission as a lens through which you view plans, objectives, and outcomes. Items that fall outside of your mission will be blurred while those that fit will be clear. Mission focus helps you better interpret data.

In 1994, Jeff Bezos, a thirty-year-old vice president of a New York investment firm with a secure future ahead of him, decided to give it all up and start a business. He believed that people would buy books through a little-known network of computers called the Internet, if buying was easy and service was customer focused. "For all of Amazon's ups and downs over the past 13 years, Bezos's strategy is one thing that hasn't changed. Customers want three things, he says: the best selection, the lowest prices, and the cheapest and most-convenient delivery"[xxxvi].

So what happened? Bezos persevered. Here is the result of his mission-focused execution using the performance of Amazon stock.

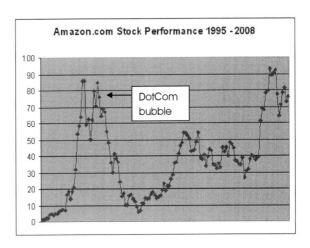

Le

Leaders energize employees

Open-book management, employee empowerment, continuous improvement, participative management, and self-directed work teams are all concepts that seek to energize employees by making them a more integral part of the workplace.
—Jack Stack

Great leaders are enthusiastic, and they transmit that enthusiasm to their employees whether they lead a church, a sports team, a nonprofit, or a for-profit company. A leader's enthusiasm comes from inner drive, belief in a vision, and confidence in their ultimate success.

It is not always easy to be enthusiastic and upbeat, but leader's continued optimism about the future and their ability to rise to these challenges energizes those who work with and for them. Think about it—if your boss completely loses enthusiasm, how much enthusiasm can you maintain?

It is not necessary to be a cheerleader to communicate enthusiasm. Leaders have different styles. You can be quietly enthusiastic through actions like publicly showing appreciation for employee efforts—that energizes. If someone is struggling, act as a mentor and help them find a solution.

Tip: Don't dampen employees' enthusiasm by complaining about external events or people—it is distracting and discouraging to team members.

What else can a leader do to share enthusiasm?
- Create a safe, trusting, work environment.
- Recognize employees for the good work they have done.
- Send clear signals you trust them by delegating, empowering, and keeping them in the know.
- Make them accountable for clearly understood outcomes.
- Share information.
- Don't hover, but be there when they need you.

If it fits your style, practice team-building exercises. Show why you believe goals are attainable with group effort. Encourage your team to try. Step in and help when things get rough. Share your enthusiasm through discussions, writing, and most importantly, through your presence.

Personal tip: Don't forget to keep yourself energized. Don't dismiss the personal value of exercise, healthy eating, and relaxation in maintaining yourself. If you are excited and energized, it becomes infectious.

Lm

Healthy management chain

Know the organization

Respect the people

Mutual goals not over-control

Open communication

Reward don't punish the messenger

Provide direction and resources

Developed forty-five hundred years ago, the management chain is a hierarchy of layered reporting and supervisory relationships. Organizations with many layers, like traditional 1950s organizations, experience lower organizational trust than the flatter organizations that became popular in the 1980s and 1990s.

What makes a management chain healthy?

- Populated with strong leadership talent (rather than subject matter experts) selected through scientific selection
- Knit together with a leadership philosophy—not a "values statement" but a common set of beliefs about how to treat employees for optimal performance
- Superior leadership development program to sharpen natural skills and significantly broaden experience
- Significant amount of the top, leadership time spent on developing future leaders
- Free flow of good and bad news up and down the chain
- Effective use of symbolic actions by top leadership

How to diagnose your own management chain: Unhealthy management chains are characterized by overcontrol. You can get a sense of the health of a management chain by observing staff meetings. Are values and behaviors ever discussed? Are ideas readily offered, accepted, and praised? Are there concrete discussions to improve operations or the work environment? Or does fear hold people back, so staff meetings are consumed with administrative detail, notices, or complaints about sister organizations?

Do's and don'ts for leaders in a healthy management chain: Conduct meetings with respect and open communication. Don't punish someone for innovative thinking. Aggressively share information and knowledge upward in the organization and down to your staff. Periodically assess the role of management within the organization to ensure the chain is helping provide direction and resources and is not just adding another layer. Make sure your staff feels comfortable sharing good news and bad news. Practice what you preach—a recent Corporate Leadership Council[xxxvii] study on high-performance leadership teams analyzed 195 potential drivers and found if executives were not good role models, there was no chance of being a top-tiered leadership organization.

Em

Empowers

Having decision-making
power

Having access to information

Having necessary resources

Having the ability to self-
initiate actions

Having support in building
new skills

Empowerment is having authority, confidence, and resources to get a task properly completed. Recent studies and surveys show empowered employees solve problems more quickly and creatively than employees forced to follow detailed procedure manuals or cumbersome chains of command. Empowerment allows you to use all the brains in an organization, not just those at the top, so the entire knowledge and experience of a team can be brought to bear on problem solving. What's more, employees who are part of decision making and quality control are more committed to executing decisions — you get buy-in.

The World Bank defines empowerment as: "the process of increasing the capacity of individuals or groups to make choices and to transform those choices into desired actions and outcomes." (See Further Reading to download and read their free book on being an empowering organization.)

When you empower employees, it implies trust in their abilities and judgment. Until the 1970s, managers told people specifically how to do their jobs and constantly watched to make sure they were doing what they were supposed to be doing. It was an adversarial relationship, which created a low-trust environment for everyone.

Highly competitive business environments and knowledge workers themselves demand a more effective, nonadversarial relationship between management and workers. Project teams empowered to get a job done are more successful and less costly than hierarchically managed workers of the past.

Strategic case study: Take the Toyota Motor Company's production lines with their famous "andon cords." At a cost of millions of dollars, any employee on the Toyota line can stop production by pulling the cord if they come across a problem. That's empowerment.

In 1990, *The Machine That Changed the World* was published — a book based on an MIT study of the future of the automobile. It provided an interesting glimpse of data from ninety auto-assembly plants around the world. Even that long ago, it was easy to see from the charts and graphs that the Japanese were doing something very different from their competitors, and what they were doing was already paying off. Rather than using mass production, the Japanese developed "lean" production which emphasized teamwork, communication, and empowerment.

At the time, most auto companies stayed with the techniques and approaches of Henry Ford's time, but Toyota had a different philosophy:

- Stop to fix problems to get quality right.
- Empower employees to continually improve "standardized practices."
- Make decisions by consensus but execute rapidly.
- Relentlessly reflect to become a learning organization.
- Grow leaders who teach this philosophy to others.

Around the time the book was published, Toyota had slightly under 50 percent of the sales of GM but received about eighteen suggestions per employees annually, while GM received less than one per employee. GM accepted 23 percent of those ideas while Toyota implemented about 80 percent. In many cases, Toyota employees implemented their own ideas. Within seventeen years, in large part because of empowered employees, Toyota surpassed GM in worldwide auto sales.

Lesson: Making sweeping decisions at the top that have enormous consequences can be quite risky, but allowing numerous small experiments at the bottom isn't.

Empowerment Benefits Everyone

*This is especially important
for government and
nonprofit organizations.*

Numbers are our friends! The best organizations use them wisely and frequently. Use relevant data to drive decisions and to help avoid wishful thinking. Of course, not all data is the same in value or accuracy. Apply the tools and processes suggested in chapters 13 (Use Tools) and 15 (Fact-Based Decision Making).

What kind of data helps drive decisions? Data that answer questions to help you understand your current situation, product or service trends, and changes in the market place will help drive decisions. Data can be time, quantity, or cost numbers. Data can also include qualitative measurements reduced to comparable numbers. For example, you can ask your customers to rate your product and services on a Likert scale from 1 to 5 or from extremely bad to exceptionally good. You can summarize and analyze customers' responses.

If you are a tailored, software-solutions manager, you need a lot of data: how much the development will cost, how long it will take to complete, and how you will measure customer satisfaction. You also want to know what your overhead rates are and your historic costs for materials, turnover, and revisions. As the project executes, you want to know if you are on target for your forecasted budget and accomplishments. Use this information to modify spending, staffing, or scheduling or customer expectations as needed.

Through skillful organization of data, you can do much more than simply get a status snapshot of your project. You can use the periodic collection of performance and cost information to look at trends and compare performance across multiple projects to understand fluctuations in individuals or teams.

You can also use data to improve decision making by focusing on information ranging from business development or new-product introductions to college recruiting. The data that helps you make these decisions is a little

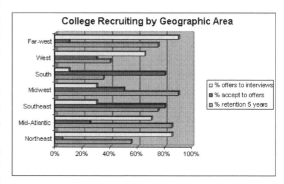

softer than project-management data because of many assumptions, uncertainties, and factors outside your control. Here is a data set from human resources to help you decide where to focus your college recruiting dollars to increase the chance of finding, employing and holding high potential employees.

By analyzing this data, you might decide to focus your college recruiting in the Midwest and the Southeast because those graduates are more likely to accept and stay than graduates from other parts of the country. The best new employees are those who accept your offer and stay with you, and data help you decide.

63

Sp

Strategically plans

Step 1: *Evaluate your business—identify five or six key areas.*

Step 2: *Make choices based on meeting your corporate vision across key value areas.*

Step 3: *Establish priorities based on current performance, goals and where you believe your efforts may have the greatest impact.*

Step 4: *Develop your action plan. "Be creative here. Don't limit yourself to what you've always done or you'll see the*

Strategic planning involves making decisions about the allocation of resources for staffing, facilities, research and development, marketing, maintenance, and other budget-line items. Strategic planning has a longer-term horizon than meeting next month's payroll or next quarter's profits and helps make your vision and your mission reality.

Tip: The best organizations mix planning with agility because the future never seems to turn out the way we predict. When the environment shifts, they aren't frozen to a static and suddenly outdated plan. Organizations in a few, rapidly changing markets pull their planning horizons down to six months. Wal-Mart does not use forecasting—just real-time decision making. This doesn't mean Wal-Mart isn't thinking strategically, however as suggested by The Economist's View[xxxviii] (October 22, 2008).

Your strategic plan will include measurable goals—your scorecard. Your strategic plan will drive the development of tactics to reach your goals. Tactics are the "what" and "how" answers to strategic planning's "why." As observed by Sun Tzu, a Chinese military expert from 500 BC, said, "Strategy without tactics is the slowest route to victory. Tactics without strategy is the noise before defeat."[xxxix]

Design tactics that use your strengths and overcome weaknesses. Also, acknowledge threats to reaching your goals and identifying opportunities—see SWOT (elements 10 and 36). In some large companies, there may be an entire department tasked with strategic planning.

Step 5: Implement and track performance using key indicators.

—Gary Lockwood

When I worked for Jack Welch at General Electric in the 1990s, Welch thought his strategic planners were too consumed with financial details rather than with competitive positioning and future markets. In effect, they were too divorced from the day-to-day reality of line managers. Welch turned strategic planning over to cross-disciplined teams of managers and later pushed the managers to interact with key customers and suppliers.

64

K

Leverage knowledge

Document experiences

The importance of culture

Share experiences through easily retrievable documents and meetings

Find out what your employees know

Provide opportunities for employees to share their knowledge

Knowledge is power. When you leverage knowledge, you can influence people, events, and decisions. As a manager and leader, you have accumulated a base of knowledge about your business, the marketplace, and human behavior, but don't forget, beyond your personal knowledge is the impressive, collective knowledge of your organization.

Definition: Knowledge is that facility of intellect that lets you apply context and experience to the interpretation of data and to see relationships among discordant or isolated pieces of information.

Remember, the best organizations leverage knowledge from everyone they can: employees, consumers, experts, and suppliers. They facilitate the identification, capture, dissemination, and use of your organization's knowledge as part of the organizational culture.

The real power of leveraging knowledge is pulling information and ideas out of employee minds, which is best accomplished in fear-free work environments. Cultures marked by caution and control are met with limited acceptance.

If you wonder how receptive your culture is to leveraging knowledge, watch how managers treat mistakes. Artifacts can also be a cultural indicator. Artifacts at the CIA include the famous CIA seal on the floor of the old headquarters building and the stars on the wall. An artifact—as simple as how many whiteboards your organization has—can give you insight into your organization's culture.

Google offers an extreme example of this: Probably the most famous was a giant white board called "The Google Master Plan" at corporate headquarters in Mountain View, California. Employees doodled and commented until the board was filled. Luckily, a picture of the board was posted on the Internet before it was erased. Finally a new board was put up and many of the comments were complaints about the removal of the first. If you Google "Google Whiteboard," you can see many of the witty comments and clever graphics done by employees on the original.

It doesn't matter how you get it done. Effectively leveraging knowledge gives your organization a significant advantage. You reach better solutions quicker with fewer mistakes. Knowledge is just as powerful as money in reaching objectives. And never forget George Santayana's seminal observation that those who do not learn from history are doomed to repeat it.

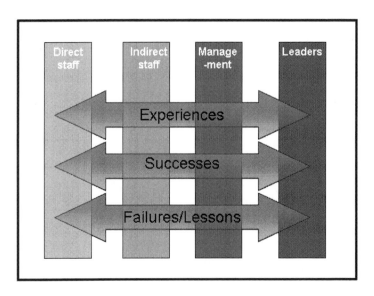

Leverage Knowledge across the Organization

65

Ag

Is agile

What agile organizations do right:

Decentralize decision making

Apply new technologies

Reuse

Collaborate

Listen to your customers

Question the status quo

As organizations strive to improve their market share and outdo successful practices of international competitors, they are searching for ways to increase agility. Agility is the ability to quickly respond to unexpected, environmental changes.

As a general rule, flatter organizations are more agile than hierarchical ones since the point of decision making and the point of information collection are closer together (i.e., communications lines are shorter). A second big factor is decision making is pushed lower.

Wal-Mart is known for incredible market agility. Store managers call in weekly about competitor's current and future sales and pricing, and decisions are made on the spot to counter them. You may also remember the speed with which they responded to the Katrina disaster.

Other agile organizations: Singapore Customs Service uses technology to enhance agility, and they can clear a ship through customs in ten minutes with electronic data interchange.

In early 2003, Nextel learned of an upcoming NASCAR sponsorship opportunity and negotiated and closed a contract in six weeks, edging out larger competitors.

The U.S. Social Security Administration is rapidly moving to e-government and shifting staff to direct service positions to increase agility in the face of the baby boomer retirement wave.

Nokia can respond within twenty-four hours to a market change anywhere in the world. Nokia's vision is to respond to market change anywhere globally within one hour.

Software projects, especially large software development efforts, are targets ripe for criticism for their inability to deliver useable products in a timely fashion. Here are three emerging prerequisites for corporate agility suggested by C. K. Prahalad and others in "The Essence of Business Agility"[xl].

1. **Access to information in context:** Information without context is of little value. Context (time, source, credibility, and other factors) becomes relevant by a specific concern or a question the manager may face that requires action.

2. **Capacity to create new knowledge and insights:** Managers

should evaluate alternative courses of action and make choices. They should solicit and consider information from a variety of sources including their employees (see element 64).

3. **Resource reconfiguration:** The rapid reconfiguration of resources may involve shifting inventories, scaling up production, reassigning staff, and stopping a failing initiative.

66

Cf

Has customer focus

Understand
Customer's Issues

Provide
Customers
Updates

Ask about Needs

Invite Customer
Participation

Share Information
on Products and
Plans

Design Processes
for Customers

Do More than the
Minimum

Ask for Feedback

Monitor Customer
Experiences

Customer is a big word. When you provide profit or nonprofit services, you'll have a widely distributed customer base that includes employees (internal customers) who receive your services and, in some cases, the community at large.

Consider their needs in the development and pricing of products by making a practice of listening to them—it is especially important to listen to internal customers (employees). You may use focus groups, and you will certainly meet with your customers and potential customers routinely.

Because you are customer-focused, you have placed personnel with true decision-making authority in charge of building and maintaining customer relationships. The salaries and bonuses of your managers include assessment of their customer focus. You strive to provide exceptional service and products. You go beyond the least common denominator. You also train your employees to focus on customers, and you serve as a role model. What does a customer-focused organization act like?

Here is an example to get you thinking:

Everyone knows someone who has sat on a runway for hours for de-icing, take off queues, FAA time limitations, maintenance difficulties, and scheduling problems. On Southwest Airlines, pilots often walk the aisles and answer questions, and flight attendants keep passengers informed about connecting flights. Some frequent-flyers even get free trip vouchers in the mail after they return home.

Southwest Airlines has an executive devoted to communicating with customers. Better yet, customer service is embedded in their corporate culture.

Customer focus is more than customer service. It involves intense, on-going analysis of the customer's experience through every stage of your product or service lifecycle. It also involves employees having deeply embedded desires to provide exceptional customer service.

67

Ur

Uses resources wisely

Applying finite resources to tasks involves some complicated trade-offs. There is always a short supply of time, talent, money, and information. Information is one of your most valuable resources— collect it from your reading, classes, employees, and customers. You can also extrapolate information from data and trend analysis.

To ensure wise resource usage, include resource requirements in your product, process, and project planning, and then view plans in combination across the organization. Use all the other elements, like element 7, Collect data, to resolve any issues before they negatively impact resources as shown in the following, terrible examples:

- The Groundnut Scheme (1946)—Hypothesis: inefficient peanut farming in what is now Tanzania can easily be overcome by adding Western equipment. Unforeseen barriers: lack of clearing equipment, floods that wiped out the single rail line, strikes, lions, crocodiles, elephants, rhinos, clay soil, lack of suitable water, hard to remove baobab trees with bees in hollow centers, inexperienced equipment operators, another flashflood, drought, and scorpions. Project cancelled in 1951 at a cost of £ 49 million.

- Daimler's buyout of Chrysler.

- In 2006, the U.S. Congress gave $500,000 for the Sparta Teapot

Museum in Sparta, North Carolina. They then followed up with $13.5 million for the International Fund for Ireland to help finance the World Toilet Summit.

Of course, you can't be "penny wise and pound foolish," either. Saving a few hundred dollars by buying a less capable computer or sharing a printer only to find that employees are less productive and time is wasted, is foolish. And never forget, people are your most valuable resource.

Tip: Money spent on training, development, and mentoring is a wise use of resources.

Guidelines on Using Resources Wisely

- Include intangible resources in calculating allocation across projects.
- Resolve conflicts in schedules over multiple projects for staff and tangible resources.
- Tie your resource allocation to your vision and goals.
- Use your resources to reward performance.
- Use your resources to find and solve problems early in the product development cycle and in the execution of processes.
- Use resources to improve performance and recognize contributions.
- Use resources to invest in your employees, including training and work environment.
- Use resources to enhance your customer's experience.
- Use tools to help visualize your resource allocation.
- Limit or remove resources from activities that do not contribute to your strategic plans and goals.

68

T

Treats employees with respect

Say thank you

Learn and use their names

Encourage them to offer their opinions and insights

Listen

Praise

Be courteous

Respect is something you earn for yourself but you owe to others.

How many of the following ways to show respect to employees do we inadvertently violate every day?

- Be honest with them.
- Share information about the organization's status and plans, trusting employees can understand and deal with both unpleasant and positive information
- Freely share your knowledge.
- Provide fair and frequent feedback.
- Listen to your employees.
- Look employees in the eye to give full attention to what they are saying.
- Remove barriers.
- Listen without judgment.
- Use employees' names when addressing them.
- Respect employees' privacy if given a confidence.
- Set clear standards.
- Show concern.
- Pay them fairly.
- Understand they have a life outside of the workplace.
- Ask their opinions.
- Expect them to do their jobs to the best of their ability and don't check up on them surreptitiously.
- Never speaking disparagingly of anyone.

Dale Carnegie's *How to Win Friends and Influence People* published in 1936 sold over 15 million copies. If you boil it down, the advice he gives is pretty simple: squelch your natural desire to be argumentative with others, and remember their names. Two simple acts of respect.

69

Cb

Collaborates

Collaboration involves working together toward a common goal. Collaboration is teamwork. We have already covered many of the core skills that allow collaboration to work successfully: improving organizational problem solving and task execution, sharing knowledge, listening, being respectful, and having decentralized decision making. Of course, when you put a team together for a specific outcome, strive to have employees with complementary skills. Effective collaboration results in more innovation, improved quality, and knowledge sharing. It's also exhilarating for the participants.

Spence's basic rules of collaboration:[xli]

- Look for common ground: find shared values, consider shared personal experiences, pay attention to and give feedback, be yourself and expect the same of others, be willing to accept differences in perception and opinions.
- Learn about others: consider their perspectives and needs, appeal to the highest motives, let others express themselves freely.
- Critique results, not people: do not waste time on personal hostility—make other people feel good and avoid criticism and put-downs.
- Give and get respect: show respect for others opinions, be considerate and friendly, put yourself in the other person's shoes, be responsive to emotions, speak with confidence but remain tactful.
- Proceed slowly: present one idea at a time, and check for understanding and acceptance of each idea before moving on to the next. Speak in an organized and logical sequence.
- Be explicit and clear: share your ideas and feelings, pay attention to nonverbal communication, speak clearly, make eye contact, and select words that have meaning for your listeners.
- Remember the five Cs of communication: clarity, completeness, conciseness, concreteness, and correctness

70

E

Streamlines processes

Streamlining processes improves operating efficiencies as well as employee quality of life. Jeremy, who works in a highly bureaucratic organization, asked, "Just what do the executives do around here? Why don't they remove barriers?" It's a good question.

Once executives commit to continual improvement rather than merely operating on autopilot, they will establish ways to understand the impact of current processes and policies on key performance indicators. They will also express urgency about changing processes to improve productivity, efficiency, and quality of life.

Advanced: Many think if you shorten the time it takes to do something, you'll increase the number of errors. The opposite is true. In the 1990s, GE's Six Sigma projects almost always reduced process times by 70 percent while reducing errors dramatically. This is because taking out steps and redundancies reduces the number of times you have the potential for losing, delaying, or mishandling paperwork or whatever else it is you are working with. Streamlined organizations run at about a 3 Sigma and above, and traditional organizations run at about a 1 Sigma or below. That translates into a great deal more rework, wasted time, and frustration for employees in traditional organizations. Since you are already paying their salary and want to use more of their brains, why not establish a top-down and bottom-up disciplined approach to cutting red tape?

How: Are you streamlining your processes? First, simplify a process whenever possible either by removing steps in the process or getting additional outcomes so you can scrap another process. To the extent possible, after you have improved processes, automate them. Collect and use performance data to measure the cost of processes and provide comparison through meaningful data when you change, add, or delete steps. Finally, the data you collect will help you control the process after you fixed it so it doesn't snap back into its original shape.

Actively solicit input from your employees to improve processes because those closest to the work know it best and will have the most useful insights into how the processes can be improved. A big lesson learned in the 1980s was that employee participation motivates them, gives them buy-in, and lets you engage more brain power for better solutions.

Tip: Look at streamlining holistically by focusing on the total cost and not the point cost of a single improvement. It may save money to purchase whatever computer is on sale when you need a new one, but that change may increase the cost of maintenance and access/storage of replacement parts.

Rules for Streamlining Processes

- Know how your processes execute, including labor hours, costs, interactions, and dependencies.
- Identify areas for streamlining based on data not assumptions or beliefs.
- Consider the entire organization's needs when making changes.
- Only solve a problem once.
- Use automation tools whenever possible.
- Solicit input from customers and staff about the impact of streamlining.
- Streamlining is a process that should be part of your constant improvement strategy.
- Review all aspect of your operation for streamlining opportunities, including workflow, paper flow, supply chain, administrative functions, training, customer service, and product development.

EXERCISES

Exercise 1
Your Future Organization

What does your future hold?

In elements 56–70, you have looked at the characteristics of a future organization that will be successful and a great place to work. Thinking about your current organization, what five things can you begin doing today to become your desired future organization?

1. _____
2. _____
3. _____
4. _____
5. _____

Exercise 2
Energizing Your Employees

Communicating and Creating Energy

When you get employees excited about your organization and what they are doing, they will energize customers and each other. Can you remember when someone who really got you motivated for a project, a cause, or an idea?

Describe the circumstances:

1. What did the leader do to get you motivated?

2. Why do you think that approach worked?

3. Did others respond the same way you did?

4. Are there any takeaways from this experience that you can apply to your current situation?

Exercise 3
Use Data to Drive Decisions

Teaching the Value of Having Data

Great organizations understand why data are important to decisions, and they use it. For this exercise, imagine that you have a new project

1. _____
2. _____
3. _____

manager – someone who has had line or direct jobs but never managed. They think they know how to do the job and are reluctant to "waste" time collecting data. How can you persuade them of the value and necessity of collecting data?

4. _____

Exercise 4
Leveraging Knowledge

Digging Out and Using Your Corporate Knowledge Assets

It is time for some out-of-the-box, creative thinking about leveraging your organization's knowledge base. Your organization wants to give back to your community, and you are tasked by your boss to help on a project to increase interest in science at a high school of your choice.

Develop your plan of attack. How do you scope the project? How can you learn about the knowledge and hidden talents of your staff? Be creative here – go beyond a questionnaire. How can you get buy-in from the staff so they will help you ferret out and use the knowledge of your colleagues? How will you organize the knowledge? How can you share the knowledge to reach the corporate objective?

Chapter 20: Higher Employee Performance

In the long run, your employees—their performance, their commitment, and their creativity—will be the force that ensures the success of your operation. You have a significant role to play in making sure employees are able and willing to give their best to the organization. You succeed at achieving higher, employee performance by facilitating, enabling, valuing, listening, and providing feedback.

The exact way you accomplish your part in this success will vary based on your organization and your skills. The core principles for higher, employee performance are fixed. It is up to you to create the environment that will help employees and ultimately make the total organization the "best place to work."

- Why you must know the strengths of individual employees for the good of the organization
- The importance of frequent feedback
- Emphasizing positive feedback makes a big difference
- How to be a non-autocratic manager
- Enabling learning
- The value of casual conversation
- Employees react to your concerns for them
- Part of positive feedback is focusing on the progress of individual employees
- Encourage learning and promote growth for individuals
- Employee's opinions are valuable to the organization
- Everyone makes mistakes—teach them to accept, learn, and move on
- The importance of understanding and showing how each employee's job helps fulfill the organization's mission
- Show your employees how their opinions count
- The importance of honesty in every interaction

Ps

Play to their strengths

Align skills to roles

Coordinate talent for effectiveness

Focus on what an employee does well

Help employees understand their talents

Organizations succeed through the effort of employees, focused by their manager's vision, guidance, and modeling. You have the power to leverage each employee's unique skills to reach your mission. When you pay attention to signals from your interactions with employees, you're able to tailor assignments to the most suitable staff members — you play to their strengths.

I once attended a Greatest Managers Conference comprised of managers who rated extremely high on Gallup's Q-12 survey in motivating high employee performance. The breaks were fascinating as these managers busily swapped best practices on how to become even better leaders. They were more successful than many managers and leaders because instead of trying to fix the weaknesses in an employee's performance, they used an employee's strengths. Great leaders intentionally make time to recognize employees as individuals, acknowledge their unique strengths, and tie those strengths to the organization's needs.

Story: Here's an example from Gallup's *Now, Discover your Strengths.*[xlii] In the late 1990s, Ralph Gonzales turned around a troubled Best Buy store in Florida. He said, "Everything comes down to knowing your people." He first watched to see if employees were people-persons or gravitated toward merchandizing. Then he looked for the smilers among the people-persons and put them in customer service or on checkout registers. He placed those with natural selling talent on the retail floor. After discovering their strengths, Gonzales analyzed how individuals wanted to be managed and adjusts his behavior accordingly. After the store became one of the best in the system, Ralph explained, "I keep watching like this, getting to know each of them. If I didn't, none of the other stuff would work."

Use a hallway meeting or even a formal review to learn the type of tasks your employees enjoy doing — those are the ones they'll usually do well. Using that insight when making task assignments allows the employee to meet their needs and apply their strengths in the best interest of the organization. Employees who believe their interests are considered and their capabilities are valued will work hard to meet your expectations.

Remember: Behavior that is a weakness in one setting is not a weakness in all settings. A detail-driven employee may not do well on a task that requires risk taking or out-of-the-box thinking, but they can be helpful balancing a highly creative person who doesn't want to be bothered with implementation specifics. Likewise, an enthusiastic go-getter may work well at the beginning of a project but flag in the end game. Use that person to generate ideas and prototyping solutions. Use your employee's strengths to benefit the organization.

Build your best organization by playing to your employee's strengths

Feedback continues the communication that began with tasking. You know that everyone responds positively to praise, and honest critique helps them do a better job. What makes you unique among your leadership and management peers is that you seek out opportunities to provide feedback—you do not just wait for someone's annual review. You know that 61 percent of American workers received no praise at work last year. Sixty-one percent! And the number one reason people leave their jobs is because they feel unappreciated (according to a Gallup survey outlined in the book, *How Full is Your Bucket?* This is not a mistake you make.

When you give feedback, either praise or constructive criticism, you are specific. You take the time to explain with details what went right or wrong. If you are giving constructive criticism, elaborate on what would have been a better behavior choice for the employee. Provide feedback as close in time to the event as possible. Although you may give praise in a public forum or through e-mail, try to give it face-to-face too. Always provide constructive criticism in a private place. Link the employee's behavior to organizational goals and mission that provide context and help the employee know how to make the right decisions in the future.

Scheduled feedback meetings are not one-way communications. Solicit feedback and information from the employee too. Listen actively to their experiences and observations. Some straight-shooting about giving feedback is provided by Gina Imperato in her *Fast Company* magazine article titled, "How to Give Good Feedback."[xliii] She provides the following guidelines which are elaborated in the article.

Guidelines for Giving Good Feedback

- Feedback is not about forms.
- Feedback delayed is feedback denied.
- Giving people a raise isn't the same as giving them feedback.
- Always get feedback on your feedback.

Pf

Emphasize positive feedback

Thoughtful
Sincere
Personal
Timely
Meaningful

Giving positive feedback that is meaningful and effective is a skill acquired through practice and thoughtful reflection. You believe in giving frequent feedback to ensure your employees understand how their performance is perceived, how it can be improved, and how it supports the organization's goals. For feedback to have the most beneficial impact, it should be detailed to events and outcomes, and it must be timely. It is nice to say, "Good job, Jim," but it is more useful to tell Jim *why* his job performance was perceived as good.

When you give feedback, practice good communication skills. Look Jim in the eye. Stop whatever else you are doing or thinking about and focus on him. You may give positive feedback individually or in a group. Because you know your employees, you know that some are embarrassed by public attention even when they appreciate being recognized. Others like to be publicly recognized and singled out for their efforts. Use your judgment about which feedback style will be most useful and appropriate.

In addition to providing immediate and meaningful, verbal feedback, also take opportunities to document good performance in the employee's record, during performance reviews, and to upper management. Do not provide positive feedback just for doing one's job, though. Coming to work on time and executing the assigned tasks is what Jim is being paid to do. If you praise trivial accomplishments, that will diminish the value of your sincere, positive feedback.

Your emphasis on positive feedback does not exclude your willingness to give constructive suggestions when warranted, but your emphasis should be on seeking out occasions for positive feedback, such as when someone has been complimented by another employee or customer, has exceeded expectations through hard work and creative problem solving, or because someone has overcome adversity to meet project or organizational goals.

Treat your employees the way you want to be treated—with respect and fairness. Many bosses don't. I surveyed five hundred people with self-described, poor or awful bosses, and in slightly over 90 percent of the cases, they described extreme, autocratic behaviors. Even more interesting, 97 percent described their job performance as much worse under these bosses than under non-autocratic bosses. Other studies point out this same tendency for autocratic bosses to drive mediocre or poor performance.

Yet, autocratic behaviors live on. Perhaps you grew up as a professional in an era when the autocratic manager was the norm. He told employees what to do; they obeyed or suffered the consequences. His fear-focused style did not make the work environment a happy place; fear can control people in the short term, but over the midterm, fear negatively affects productivity and commitment.

Case study: In the late 1990s, a senior government manager we'll call Lester was known for his autocratic management style. He was blunt, confrontational, and widely disliked by his employees. Lester told his employees, "Your main job is to keep us out of the newspapers. You aren't my main priority."

He was vicious in battling other managers for resources. He abused his employees, but as is often the case with autocratic leaders, if you were on Lester's good side, you did quite well. A small group of sycophants nested closely around him.

Lester got into a dispute with a Congressman who threatened to do away with his unit. Stopping for just a moment, how would you handle this with your employees? Lester's solution: he called his employees together and told them they should check their personnel files and prepare for the worst. He rented buses, which shuttled employees twice daily to the records depository two hours away. Then Lester disappeared for three weeks. Part of the time, he was battling on the Hill, but he never bothered to communicate any of this to employees. All work stopped.

Epilogue: The unit was not disbanded after all. Lester left government management a year later. Today, the unit performs very well and does invaluable work. The buses no longer shuttle.

Modern world's worst autocrat: In Moscow, selected visitors were shepherded into Comrade Stalin's office. Stalin would studiously ignore the person and continue to work at his desk. The visitor stood quaking in absolute silence. The story goes that Stalin would not look up until they wet their pants.

In the late 1980s, my favorite building in Moscow was the Stalinist-style Hotel Moskva. When I walked by it, I knew something was wrong, but I had to scrutinize the facade to see the inappropriate imbalance of moldings, roof lines, and windows on the right and left sides of the fourteen-story monstrosity. Reportedly, the architect went into Stalin's office to show two alternatives, and Stalin absentmindedly initialed both sets of plans. The architect and Stalin's staff didn't know what to do: the "brilliant genius of humanity" never made mistakes, so they couldn't go back to clarify which plan he really approved. The architect did the only thing he could do; he built the building with both sets of plans.

Remember, under autocratic control, whole organizations can become like Stalin's hotel. Sadly, in 2004, this breathtaking monument to autocratic management practices was finally torn down.

Non-autocratic managers achieve corporate objectives by getting buy-in from the employees. The organization's environment encourages the free flow of ideas and communication among all personnel — clerical staff, field personnel, project professionals, and project managers. Staff are encouraged to discuss problems, issues, and concerns. Non-autocratic managers share information, they solicit input, they provide the tools to get the job done, and they recognize and appreciate the contributions of every employee.

E

Enable them to learn their jobs

Orientation
Task training
Tools training
Process training
Skills training
Problem solving

No matter how well trained a new employee is when he or she arrives at the front door of your organization, he or she still has a lot to learn about working within your organization. Provide an environment that fosters learning through initial orientation, ongoing training, mentoring, modeling, and frequent feedback. Know that learning a job in your company is more than mastering the tasks to be performed — it includes learning how the organization does things and why they are done that way. Learning requires understanding the culture, the organization's mission, and its vision of the future.

As a leader and manager, you not only support on-the-job learning, you enable it. Quoting Jack Welch, retired CEO and chairman of General Electric, in an interview with Janet Lowe, "The desire and ability of an organization to continuously learn from any source, anywhere, and to rapidly convert this learning into action is its ultimate competitive advantage."

Learning involves changing behaviors. There will be practice sessions and feedback to hone and shape performance. As employees learn, they will sometimes make mistakes that can serve as examples for further learning. This learning-from-mistakes occurs when you enable staff through feedback to understand what happened and why. Enable learning by structuring a supportive work environment that includes access to information, demonstration, formal training, and frequent feedback. Provide opportunities to learn. Encourage interaction with colleagues and time for reflection on experiences.

Guidelines for Enabling Learning

- Build learning into regular work environment.
- Expect employees to practice new skills and provide feedback on their performance.
- Expect continual learning and reward it.
- Tailor training to an individual's most effective learning style.
- Provide tools to support learning.
- Expect your senior people to be trainers and mentors.
- Align individual learning with project and organizational goals.
- Spend time being a teacher and mentor, and enhance your own coaching skills.
- Practice what you preach, and be a learner all the time.

The difference between a casual conversation with your employee and a meeting is like the difference between a pick-up game of basketball and a tournament. If you are playing in a tournament, you and the other team are adversaries. You wear your game face, and you do not fraternize with the opposing team before the game—your mindset is "us against them." In a pick-up game, you don't worry so much about preparation. You kid around and have fun, and it is less about beating the other team than about playing.

In a casual conversation with an employee, remove the adversarial aura—that sense of being called into the principal's office. What is the advantage of this approach? The employee does not need to be defensive—after all, it is just talking. He may reveal more information about his job, his accomplishments, and his concerns. Use this opportunity to chat about what is going on in the organization, where you think things are heading, or how you want a task done. Speak off-the-cuff, as opposed to in an organized, perhaps even documented, formal meeting.

You may be surprised to find that your employees remember better what you say to them in casual conversation than in the formal meetings and annual state-of-the-organization presentations. Their ability to listen and understand is heightened when they are not distracted by worrying about how they look, defending a position, or constructing what they are going to say next. Casual conversations are psychologically safer—employees spend less emotional energy defending and protecting and more energy listening and talking.

where ...   their office/cube

by the copier

parking lot   hallway

cafeteria   elevator

refreshment area

Make time for casual conversation

Safety
Benefits
Customized
Health
Environment
Response
Advocacy
Compensation

Your employees have lives outside of work that influence the quality of their work efforts and vice versa. They appreciate when you take time to show an interest in them as people and not just automaton contributors to the bottom line. One of the ways you show your concern is by asking personalized questions that reflect your knowledge of their interests, such as, "Joe, how did Sammy do in the softball tournament?" or "Mary, how's your Mom doing?" This simple exchange tells the employee that you know about their lives, and you care enough to follow up on previously communicated information.

Show your concern in the way you couch expectations that require your employees to go beyond the normal or average work routine. When there is a project deadline that will require hours of overtime to meet the schedule, acknowledge that fact and reiterate why this project and their time is important to the organization. You may even go out of your way to see them as they come in early or leave late and thank them for their efforts, or you may provide special treats, such food and drink served in common areas, to acknowledge the extra efforts being made.

In 2007, the *Seattle Times* posted a brief story about a woman highly concerned about getting her daughter to that traumatic, first day of first grade. She anxiously approached her boss at Monterey Gourmet Foods, Eric Eddings, and asked about coming in late. Some bosses would refuse, but Eddings answered, "That's important. You should be there for her. Your family should be No. 1."

Quick quiz: You don't have to offer time off to show concern. Concern can be shown by the way you react on the job everyday. Here's a quick quiz:

A problem developed within the workforce, and here's how five supervisors reacted:

- Frank did nothing.
- Bill conducted a survey.
- Mary conducted a survey and shared the results with her employees.
- Jim conducted a survey, shared the results with his employees, and then listened to their reactions to the survey results.
- Laura conducted a survey, shared the results with her employees, listened to their reactions to the survey results, and encouraged them to implement solutions to the issues raised in the survey.

Question: Who collected more "showing concern points?" Who solved the root problems?

Answer: Laura. She tied four other elements together to show concern: element 7, Collect data; element 106, Share; element 21, listen; and element 61, Empowerment. Finally, by successfully tying these elements together to fix the problem instead of fixing blame (element 115), she treated employees with respect (element 68).

Final tip: You can do large things and small things to show concern. For example, you may add counseling support for employees, an exercise center or fitness club membership, on-site medical screenings, health and wellness classes, or you may do any number of other little things with the common message "we are concerned about you."

You do all of this because you genuinely care about the people who work for you. The benefit to the organization is that employees reciprocate with loyalty, productivity, and commitment.

96

Pg

Focus on their progress

The journey of a thousand miles begins with one step.

Set goals for each employee that reflects both their career interests and the needs of the organization. Remember, they do not reach the best performance they are capable of immediately. They reflect, they learn, and they improve. Do not wait until they are as good as the best before you acknowledge their accomplishments. Watch, measure, and reward their progress.

The same is true when you are helping an employee remove a behavior that is counterproductive. Like breaking any bad habit, one rarely succeeds going cold turkey. As a manager, provide feedback on areas that need improvement and make suggestions on interim steps or partial successes that you will be hoping to see. If, for example, an employee is chronically late turning in reports, your progress goal may be only having one late report every month instead of no late reports ever. Of course, the longer-term goal is no late reports ever, but if "no late reports ever" is the only acceptable behavior for an employee who is almost always late with his or her reports, it may be asking too much too soon. Habits need to be changed, and that takes time. Focus on their progress in reaching the long-term goal and reward them for getting closer to the desired, end result.

In learning new job skills, work with the direct supervisor, training specialists, and the employee to identify the required steps toward skill mastery. When you break a skill into smaller, subskills, you set up an environment where the employee can experience success and be recognized. This is a principle of weight-loss programs: If the only success criterion is losing fifty pounds, that goal can take so long to achieve that one gives up along the way. But if the goal is two pounds this week, that is attainable, and the person receives an emotional boost from their progress.

Practice tangible measurement of group progress by posting charts of a reduction in errors, on-time deliveries, or fewer accidents. Although reminiscent of grade-school gold stars, reminding everyone of the long-term goals and showing the progress being made over time makes everyone feel like their behavior and performance matters.

97

Lg

Encourage learning and growing

Because you believe in the importance of learning, model the desired behavior by taking classes, attending seminars, and reading professional journals. Seek out new and challenging jobs. Just as important as your commitment to personal learning is ensuring that your employees learn and grow. Facilitate this by providing resources for learning and incentives that encourage, provoke, and reward those who improve their skills. Recognize and encourage on-the-job training, formal training, mentoring, and coaching.

Within your organization, help create an environment that not only encourages learning but also supports it. Consider implementing a knowledge management system that records, indexes, and makes available to everyone documents, manuals, lessons learned, trade articles, and formal training materials. You know that timely training assures better retention than learning that is far removed from practice, so provide just-in-time training.

When a new process or tool is being made available, you invest in training staff on its use. Encourage peer-to-peer training with one employee providing instruction to others because of skills they developed and practiced. That training may be informal—someone stops by and provides instruction—or it can be more formal as part of a staff meeting or brown-bag lunch. Encourage this knowledge sharing by modeling it, soliciting it, and rewarding those who work to make it part of everyday corporate life.

Encourage learning from your customers too. By knowing that customers and potential customers spend resources to understand their company's needs, you learn from them. Another secret about a learning organization you should share with your employees is how they can learn from competitors. Encourage your employees to track the competition and understand what they are doing to differentiate themselves from your organization. From these observations, along with your knowledge of your customers and market needs, you can learn to make your organization more productive and profitable.

Finally, encourage growth not only through structured learning activities but also by providing stretch jobs and suggesting growth goals during performance reviews and staff meetings.

98

Vo

Value their opinions

Ask
Listen actively
Write it down
Give feedback
Make it easy
Take action

One thing you have learned along the way about your management and leadership position is that you do not and cannot have all the answers. You are always delighted with the creative problem solving and new ideas that come from those around you. Because you know that each employee brings their unique take on new ideas and processes as well as problem solving strategies, actively solicit their input. Value their opinions because you know their experiences and perspective are different than your own, and they bring unique ideas, solutions, and suggestions to a discussion. Remember, consensus and buy-in are more likely to happen if everyone feels part of the process—if they can see they make a difference.

Establish procedures to share information upward in the organization. Ask for feedback and ideas—this is not just an exercise for you. The time that you put into designing the survey instruments and the time you allocate to collecting employee input is a demonstration of your belief in the value of your staff's opinions. You listen and know that there is a strong correlation between employee buy-in and profitability. You also know that out there where the rubber meets the road is a tremendous reservoir of experience and knowledge that can make your organization more effective.

The way your employees know you value their opinions is by the feedback you provide to them. First, react to the individual. If someone takes the time to communicate their thoughts on a proposed process or to suggest a solution to a nagging problem, respond to their suggestion, and let them know you appreciate their participation. You may choose to take the idea under consideration, you may study its impact by collecting more data, you may implement it, or you may believe you cannot implement it. Whatever your response, let the contributor know they made a difference.

When employee opinions are collected in formal processes, such as employee surveys, you communicate findings and proposed actions with everyone. Because you value the opinions of your employees, let them know how their opinion impacted the way you do business. Practice an open style of communication that encourages employees to share observations and suggestions. Walk around and talk with them to collect their insights and experiences. Listen actively and give feedback in a timely way.

99

A

Accept their mistakes

No one likes to make mistakes. Mistakes make people feel inadequate, embarrassed, a failure, or just stupid. None of those reactions are productive ways to move forward. You know that mistakes happen. Some of those mistakes are made in ignorance, others by execution failure, or just a set of circumstances that combine to cause a small mistake to significantly impact an outcome. You have learned how to help people use their mistakes to improve later performance. And, you teach them how to learn from the mistakes of others.

The key to success in dealing with mistakes is that accepting them as part of the learning process. Do not see mistakes as a character flaw or an unrecoverable problem, but help your employees accept that a mistake was made, determine what should be done to ameliorate the consequences, and most importantly what can be learned from the mistake by the individual, the team, and the organization. Also communicate that not all failures in execution are caused by mistakes.

Model dealing with mistakes in your own behavior. You should constantly review the feedback that the world, your customers, and your staff provide about your actions. Be scrupulously honest with yourself and others about what you did, could have done, and should have done. Determine what to do next time based on what you learn. Making mistakes does not make you a failure or a bad person. One positive result of accepting mistakes is that your staff tries tactics that they might otherwise be afraid to try because of fear of failure. Employees acknowledge mistakes rather than covering them up or blaming someone else. And, your organization is constantly improving because you use what you learn from mistakes to be more effective in the future.

100

Wm

Link their work to the mission

Screen your decisions and plans through the filter of your organization's mission. Your mission statement captures the nature of the organization and its vision for the future. Employees, especially those who are relatively new or perhaps not in positions of authority are not always clear how their tasks and performance tie into the bigger picture, so you make a point of recognizing that link and reinforcing it frequently.

Use stories during meetings and in your communications that reflect the association between performance and mission. Tie individual behaviors and role expectations to goals and objectives. Strive to communicate that no task is irrelevant or unimportant. Expect the intermediate supervisors to provide the same message during their more frequent contacts with staff. Demonstrate how tasks relate to the organization's mission by performing the tasks along with the employees.

One way you show the links between individual tasks and the broader organization mission and goals is through visual representations of tactics and objectives grouped within various aspects of the mission. Emphasize the importance of how an employee performs their tasks so consonance with the mission is exemplified. Below is a list of management and leadership opportunities to link the work of individuals to the organization's mission:

Opportunities to Link Tasks to Mission

- **Interviews** — talk about the organization's mission and how the job someone is being considered to fill fits within the mission.
- **Orientation** — emphasize the relationship between the assigned tasks and the company's vision, long-term goals, and short-term objectives.
- **Annual planning briefings** — include how their performance directly impacts the overall organizational goals and mission.
- **Performance reviews** — reinforce the link between individual tasks and corporate mission.
- **Feedback** — relate their performance to the mission and goals.
- **Process improvement** — couch the reasons you have chosen this course of action as it relates to the organization's mission.
- **Validate** — ensure employees understand the relationship between their individual assignments and the corporate mission.
- **Stories and visualization techniques** — illustrate the importance of each individual and their job in meeting the corporate mission and goals.

101

0c

Let their opinions count

It's about respect for employee's . . .

Ideas

Brains

Let your staff know that their opinions count by collecting them, reflecting them in decision making, and by providing feedback on actions and plans that show the role their opinions played in driving decisions. Although you may collect annual feedback from your employees using a traditional survey method that is only one way you show employees that their input is important to the organization.

You also ask. When you are practicing management by walking around or meeting with staff in small groups or individually, you ask for their opinions. You listen, you make notes, and you engage them in an honest dialogue about their perceptions and ideas. When an employee provides reasoned and well-intended feedback, acknowledge it. You may also forward it to higher management along with your comments. If you do, copy the individual, so they know what you thought and what you did with their input. In your organization's newsletter or other communication vehicles, you may have a section for staff opinions. All employees are encouraged to share their opinions.

Value negative opinions as much as positive ones, perhaps even more. In some instances, you may choose to have formal opinion assessments conducted anonymously to cover the few employees who have carry-over concerns from a previous employer about your real interest in their opinions and your assurances that the process is investigative not punitive. Part of encouraging the sharing of opinions is not punishing the messenger.

Your organization cannot afford to ignore or underutilize the collective experience and opinions of your employees.

You know that employees who feel part of the planning and decision-making process feel valued and are more likely to contribute the best they have to offer when it comes time for implementation. Employees who feel valued are also more likely to stay with the organization. There is no area of the company that does not benefit from collecting the opinions of employees about all aspects of the organization's activities.

You won't necessarily change the way you do business because of the opinions of your employees, but you value their input enough to listen and honestly consider making changes because of their suggestions. The organization benefits from their perspective, experience, and insights.

102

Ho

Are honest

Being honest is a lot more than not lying. Honesty involves telling the entire story, not just telling the truth about the parts you want to tell. Dishonesty can be a error of commission or omission. You are honest because you believe that is the right way to behave and also because you know that practiced honesty is returned in kind. When you ask for status or information from your employees, you do not want cherry-picked data or biased reporting. You want and need honesty to make the best decisions.

With yourself

Honesty includes consideration and reasoned judgment—applying analysis and data as well as values. Practicing honesty means that when you are aware of an issue, you confront it. If you have a concern, seek all the data you need to understand and resolve the concern. Strive to be as honest with yourself as you are with others.

With your employees

Being honest in your dealings with customers gives your organization a trustworthy reputation. You cannot buy a good reputation—you earn it—and you can lose it quickly through deceitful practices. You also know that you must be proactive in your honesty. If there is a problem,

With your customers

you should be the one to call it to the attention of a customer, a board member, or an employee. Being honest doesn't means waiting until someone else discovers the problem and then, admitting it. Nor should you punish someone for being honest. When you receive bad news that

In negotiations

accurately reflects the situation on a project or with personnel, a product, or a customer, strive to find out what has happened and why.

In advertising

The newspapers are filled with stories of managers and politicians who have not demonstrated full honesty in their dealing with their employees, their customers, the public, or their own, senior management. Examples that come quickly to mind include Tyco, Martha Stewart, Enron, WorldCom, and Big Tobacco—it's a long list, but there are also stories about forthright managers who behave with

In responding to problems and mistakes

honesty and integrity. In his 2005 book, *How Honesty Pays: Restoring Integrity to the Workplace,* Charles E. Watson provides many examples of honest managers faced with difficult times who applied their core value of honesty in developing and executing their response. He cites stories of honesty, integrity, and courage about such notables as Jim Casey of UPS, George Schaefer of Caterpillar Tractor, Charles Lazarus of Toys "R" Us, and Gertrude Boyle of Columbia Sportswear.

EXERCISES

Exercise 1
The Strengths of Your Employees

Your employees have strengths that you need to make your business successful. Their strengths may be technical, thinking and reasoning, or interpersonal skills. Pick three of your employees for this thought experiment. List their strengths and how you know this to be true. Think out of the box – do not limit this experiment to only your work interactions with them.

How well do you know your employees?

Name:

Observed Strengths	Reported Strengths

Name:

Observed Strengths	Reported Strengths

Name:

Observed Strengths	Reported Strengths

Exercise 2
Nonautocratic Management

You are not an autocratic manager, but many; otherwise exceptional managers may fall into an autocratic style when time and cost pressures increase. Can you think of three examples when you or another manager became an autocrat? Is there a way to stop this from happening?

Describe the circumstances and the observed, autocratic behavior. What happened as a result?

1.

2.

3.

Exercise 3
Enabling

Give four examples of current or planned enabling activities:

As your organization grows and prospers, probably the most important thing you can do to ensure future success is to enable your employees to do the best jobs they can. Beyond the items suggested in element 93, what have you done or could you do to more effectively enable your employees?

_____

_____

_____

_____

Exercise 4
Linking Work Activities to the Mission

Map four daily activities or tasks to the mission, and show how exceptional performance makes a difference.

It is important that you be able to link the work of each employee to the mission of the organization. It is important for the organization and important for the employee. Pick three or four positions within your organization – pick ones that could be difficult to directly link to the mission because they are far removed from the decision makers. For each position or job, create a map and a strategy to communicate that to the employee.

Daily task	Related Mission Statement	Impact

THE LEADERSHIP TOP TEN:

USING THE PERIODIC TABLE TO GET RESULTS

Leadership is made up of lots of simple elements, which perhaps is why we so often forget them. So the Periodic Table is designed to help you remember all the powerful elements of leadership. There are lots of important elements like element 3 (Listen) and element 24 (Delegate), but there are a few that are absolutely crucial. Here are the top ten:

10) **Humor** (element 1) — this one seems easy but isn't when you are in the direct line of fire as a leader. It has two pieces: (1) keep your sense of humor to reduce your stress and (2) allow your subordinates to enjoy themselves. You don't have to tell jokes and be a clown, just allow a safe environment where employees can enjoy themselves and laugh. That's all humor is. The mission gets done more effectively this way.

9) **Consistency** (element 12) — this is trickier than you think. The element description says "Be consistent, transparent, predictable." The dilemma is that this is in the mind of the beholder. You aren't the beholder — the employees are. This is a very difficult element because while you think you are being consistent, they may misinterpret your behaviors as being a little erratic. That's why you have to get feedback by listening (element 21) and asking for input (element 55).

8) **Fair and frequent feedback** (element 90) — over the last eight years, this one keeps popping up as number one, two, or three in importance in studies done on morale, retention, and employee performance. There is something important to employees about finding out how they are doing and how they fit in with the big picture. This isn't the old, annual tell-them-what's-wrong-with-them; it's the new, positive let-them-know-how-they-are-doing and how they can improve even more.

7) **Recognize your shortcomings** (element 87) — this is another tough one because of the cognitive biases we all cart around as ego protection mechanisms (yes, including you and me). Bad leaders are not self-aware while good leaders are. In a bit of a paradox, people trust you more if you are aware of your faults and ask for their help in covering your flanks. The defensive person who puts on a false façade of perfection is never trusted and can't become a great leader.

6) **Get employees involved** (element 48) — employees love it when they feel their opinions count. We all work harder if we think it's our own ideas we're implementing. This concept shows up on the Gallup Q12 as question seven, so you can see the results for your own

workgroup from the last survey. Getting employees involved has a huge impact on mission performance.

5) **Selection** (element 106)—at first glance, it may seem odd that this is one of the most important elements, but selection is extremely important. Popular literature says the primary executive role is to develop future leaders, but that's really only secondary to *selecting* the right people with the right talents in the first place. If you are a supervisor, let people play to their strengths—for example, ascertain who is good at details and assign them to positions where that matters. Visionaries and "idea people" perform best in other roles in your organization.

The OSS invented advanced scientific selection assessments in World War II, and now a few private-sector companies provide these services. If you are an executive, follow the OSS's lead and use scientific selection as an additional step before selecting anyone for a supervisory or management position.

4) **Accountability and Empowerment** (elements 74 and 61)—neither of these elements is worth much by themselves, but if we fuse them together, we have a powerful compound. New studies show if you can push empowerment and accountability as far as you can, you get a high-performing organization. Be careful however—accountability is not the nineteenth century version of whipping the troops; it's simply making sure employees know the appropriate job boundaries. How much can I innovate? Can I experiment? Once employees know the boundaries, provide simple metrics to monitor progress.

3) **Motivating employee performance**—look under the Rare Earth Elements at the bottom of the chart and you see the most important group: "To motivate employees, ensure that:" followed by a string of fourteen, high-powered elements from number 89 to 102. Collectively, these maximize employee performance. They are what motivate you and the people who work for you. They deliver employee performance, which is the biggest part of mission performance. If you really believe in your mission, practice the fourteen vital elements in this group daily.

2) **Inspire, Improve, Implement**—see how all the elements are clumped into three giant families? The family on the far right, Implement, is the essence of management or getting the mission done. Inspiration, the family on the far left, is what leadership is all about—inspiring people to change direction or accomplish more. The family in the middle is Improve, which is using the family on the left, Inspire, to change the way we Implement. Improvement involves trimming bureaucracy and finding more efficient and less-stressful ways to do things. All three of these are critical for well-performing units.

1) **Trust** — look under the eighteen columns or groups, and you'll see a green line stretching across the chart titled "Trust." Trust is the foundation for great leadership. When employees trust you, they accept your vision and direction. You are a great leader when others perceive you as both trustworthy and trusting.

Further Reading

Chapter 1:

Phillips, D. *Lincoln on Leadership: Executive Strategies for Tough Times*. Business Plus, 1993.

Seligman, M. *Learned Optimism: How to Change Your Mind and Your Life*. New York: Random House, 2006.

Vaugn, S. *Half Empty, Half Full: Understanding the Psychological Roots of Optimism*. Harvest Books, 2001.

Quint Careers."Work Life Balance Quiz." Quint Careers.
http://www.quintcareers.com/work-life_balance_quiz.html. (accessed December 8, 2008)

Roy Posner. "The Power of Personal Values".
http://gurusoftware.com/Gurunet/Personal/Topics/Values.htm. (accessed December 8, 2008)

Chapter 2:

Ambrose, S. *Eisenhower*. New York. Simon & Schuster, 1991.

Coffman, E. *The Regulars: The American Army, 1898–1941*. Belknap Press of Harvard University Press, 2007.

Collins, J. *Good to Great: Why Some Companies Make the Leap ... and Others Don't*. Collins Business, 2001.

Kennedy, J. *Profiles in Courage*. New York: HarperCollins, 2003.

Kitfield, J. *Prodigal Soldiers: How the Generation of Officers Born of Vietnam Revolutionized the American Style of War*. Dulles, Virginia: Potomac Books Inc, 1997.

McCain, J. *Why Courage Matters: The Way to a Braver Life*. New York: Random House, 2004.

Miller, W. *The Mystery of Courage*. Cambridge, Massachusetts: Harvard University Press, 2000.

Olson, L. *Troublesome Young Men: The Rebels Who Brought Churchill to Power and Helped Save England*. New York: Farrar, Straus and Giroux, 2007.

Rich, B. *Skunk Works: A Personal Memoir of My Years of Lockheed*. Back Bay Books, 1996.

Soloman, B. and David Felder at the North Carolina State University Self Test on Learning Styles.available at: http://www.engr.ncsu.edu/learningstyles/ilsweb.html (accessed December 5, 2008.

Weekes, R. "Wanted: Leaders with Courage." http://www.leader-values.com/content/detail.asp?ContentDetailID=330. (accessed December 8, 2008)

Starcevich, M. "Quiz on Leadership Trustworthiness: How Far Can They Throw You?" http://www.coachingandmentoring.com/Quiz/trustworthiness.htm. (accessed December 8, 2008)

Chapter 3:

Booher, D. *Communicate with Confidence*. New York: McGraw-Hill, 1994.

Burley-Allen, M. *Listening: The Forgotten Skill: A Self-Teaching Guide*. Hoboken, New Jersey: John Wiley & Sons, 1995.

Peters, T. *In Search of Excellence: Lessons from America's Best-Run Companies*. New York: HarperCollins, 2006.

Slater, R. *The GE Way Fieldbook: Jack Welch's Battle Plan for Corporate Revolution*. New York: Tata McGraw–Hill, 1999.

"Becoming a Better Business Listener." http://www.businesslistening.com/listening_skills.php. (accessed December 8, 2008)

Chapter 4:

Bridges, W. *Managing Transitions*. New York: Perseus Publishing, 2003.

Kotter, J. *Leading Change*. Harvard Business School Press, 1996.

Bell, C. 2000. Managing by wandering around. *The Journal for Quality and Participation*, (Winter), available at http://findarticles.com/p/articles/mi_qa3616/is_200001/ai_n8893349. (accessed December 8, 2008)

"Off-sites that Work from Harvard Business Review." http://www.smartmeetings.com/issues/january-2007/articles/off-sites-that-work. (accessed December 8, 2008)

Pacelli, L. "Team Building with a Purpose." http://us.deskdemon.com/pages/us/meeting/teambuilding. (accessed December 8, 2008)

Can this off-site be saved? 2001. *Fast Company*, (September). Available online at http://www.fastcompany.com/magazine/51/offsite.html. (accessed December 8, 2008)

Survey Monkey is a service which can be found at: http://www.surveymonkey.com.

Chapter 5:

Chang, R. *The Passion Plan at Work: Building a Passion-Driven Organization*. Hoboken, New Jersey: Jossey-Bass of John Wiley& Sons, 2001.

Maxwell, J. *The 21 Indispensable Qualities of a Leader: Becoming the Person Others Will Want to Follow*. Nashville: Thomas Nelson Publisher, 1999.

Vogan, P. "5 Keys Traits of Great Leaders." http://www.entrepreneur.com/management/leadership/leadershipcolumnistpattyvogan/article163590.html. (accessed December 8, 2008)

Small Business Notes. http://www.smallbusinessnotes.com/planning/mission.html. (accessed December 8, 2008)

"The Importance of Vision." October 29, 2007.
http://discussionleader.hbsp.com/mayo/2007/10/the_importance_of_vision.html.
(accessed December 8, 2008)

Chapter 6:

Baldoni, J. *Great Motivation Secrets of Great Leaders*. New York: McGraw-Hill, 2004.
Eichenwald, K. *Conspiracy of Fools*. New York: Doubleday Broadway Publishing Group, 2005.
Laird, M. W. "Knowledge Sharing: A Perspective from Xerox—The Document Company."
http://www.aaas.org/spp/yearbook/2000/ch14.pdf. (accessed December 8, 2008)
Bobrow, D. G. and Jack Whalen. "Community Knowledge Sharing in Practice: The Eureka
Story."
http://www.parc.xerox.com/research/projects/commknowledge/EurekaReflections.pdf.
(accessed December 8, 2008)

Chapter 7:

Covey, S. *The Seven Habits of Highly Effective People*. Free Press, 2004.
Berkun, S. "Learning from Your Mistakes." http://www.scottberkun.com/essays/44-how-
to-learn-from-your-mistakes/. (accessed December 8, 2008)

Chapter 8:

Smith, D. *Make Success Measurable!: A Mindbook-Workbook for Setting Goals and Taking Action*.
Hoboken, New Jersey: John Wiley & Sons, 1999.
"Building a Common Outcome Framework to Measure Nonprofit Performance." December
2006. Developed by the Urban Institute and the Center for What Works. Available at
http://www.urban.org/UploadedPDF/411404_Nonprofit_Performance.pdf. (accessed
December 8, 2008)
"How to Measure Performance." A handbook of techniques and tools from the U.S.
Department of Energy. http://www.orau.gov/pbm/documents/handbook1a.html.
(accessed December 8, 2008)

Chapter 9:

Ambrose, S. *Eisenhower*. Simon & Schuster, 1991.
Baker, D., Cathy Greenberg, and Collins Hemingway. *What Happy Companies Know*. Saddle
River, New Jersey: Prentice Hall, 2006.
Cunningham, C. and Marcus Buckingham. *First Break All the Rules*. New York: Simon &
Schuster, 1999.

Drucker, P. *The Practice of Management*. Collins Business, 2006.

Rich, B. *Skunkworks: A Personal Memoir of My Years at Lockheed*. Back Bay, 1996.

Check out interesting white papers under "Faculty and Research" at the Center for Creative Leadership's Web site: http://www.ccl.org. (accessed December 8, 2008)

Some blogs are little more than information pollution, but there are some great ones as well on rather narrow topics. For example, if you are looking for current thinking under disciplined improvement approaches, see curiouscatblog.net.

Chapter 10:

Noone, D. *Creative Problem Solving*. Hauppauge, NY: Barron's Education, 1998.

Chapter 11:

Marcus, S. *Minding the Store*. Denton, Texas: University of North Texas Press, 1997.

Sewell, C. *Customers For Life: How To Turn That One-Time Buyer Into a Lifetime Customer*. Currency Press, 2002.

Dee, B. 2007. "Essential Elements of Effective Complaint Handling" http://www.accc.gov.au/content/index.phtml/itemId/95997. (accessed December 8, 2008)

"Complaint Management and Problem Resolution." http://www.dhhs.state.nc.us/cstf/intranet/article_complaintmanage.pdf. (accessed December 8, 2008)

Chapter 12:

Bernstein, P. *Against the Gods: The Remarkable Story of Risk*. Hoboken, New Jersey: John Wiley & Sons, 1998.

Damodaran, A. *Strategic Risk Taking: A Framework for Risk Management*. Wharton School Publishing, 2007.

"10 Mistakes Managers Make During Job Interviews by Business Net." http://www.bnet.com/2403-13068_23-52950.html?promo=713&tag=nl.e713. (accessed December 8, 2008)

Kottolli, A. "Common Mistakes in Managing Virtual Project Teams." http://arunkottolli.blogspot.com/2007/01/common-mistakes-in-managing-virtual.html. (accessed December 8, 2008)

Berkun, S."How to Learn From Your Mistakes." http://www.scottberkun.com/essays/44-how-to-learn-from-your-mistakes/. (accessed December 8, 2008)

See the Army's Lesson Learned Center at http://call.army.mil. (accessed December 8, 2008)

Chapter 13:

Pande, P. and Holpp, L. *What is Six Sigma?* New York: McGraw-Hill, 2002.

"How to Map a Process." www.odgroup.com/articles/PMap3.pdf. (accessed December 8, 2008)

"Process Mapping and Flow Charting from Six Sigma."
http://www.isixsigma.com/tt/process_mapping/. (accessed December 8, 2008)

"A Guide to Process Mapping."
http://www.cps.gov.uk/Publications/finance/process_mapping.html. (accessed December 8, 2008)

"How to make a Pareto Chart." http://www.asq.org/learn-about-quality/cause-analysis-tools/overview/pareto.html. (accessed December 8, 2008)

Chapter 14:

Cooper, R. *The Other 90%: How to Unlock Your Vast Untapped Potential for Leadership and Life.* Crown Business Publishing Group, 2001.

Surowiecki, J. *The Wisdom of Crowds.* New York: Doubleday, 2004.

Ashkensa, R. December 1, 2007. Simplicity-minded management. *Harvard Business Review.* Available online at
http://harvardbusinessonline.hbsp.harvard.edu/hbsp/hbr/articles/article.jsp?articleID=R0712H&ml_action=get-article&print=true. (accessed December 8, 2008)

He uses element 32 to break through layers of complexity found in very large organizations.

"The 14 Principles of the Toyota Way." http://www.si.umich.edu/ICOS/Liker04.pdf. (accessed December 8, 2008)

"No Satisfaction at Toyota." http://www.fastcompany.com/magazine/111/open_no-satisfaction.html. (accessed December 8, 2008)

Chapter 15:

Stephen Hale "How to Manage Data Badly."
http://www.epa.gov/emap/html/pubs/docs/imdocs/howto1.pdf and
http://www.epa.gov/emap/html/pubs/docs/imdocs/howto2.pdf (accessed December 8, 2008) A tongue-in-cheek contribution from EPA.

Chapter 16:

Anderson, E. *Growing Great Employees.* Penguin Group, 2006.

Atwater, L. *Leadership, Feedback and the Open Communications Gap.* London: Taylor and Francis Group, 2008.

Nelson, B. *1001 Ways to Reward Employees.* New York: Workman Publishing, 2005.

Spitzer, D. *Transforming Performance Management: Rethinking the Ways to Measure and Drive Corporate Success.* Available from Amazon at:
http://www.amazon.com/s/ref=nb_ss_gw?url=search-alias%3Dstripbooks&field-keywords=Transforming+Performance+Management%3A+Rethinking+the+Ways+to+Mea sure+and+Drive+Corporate+Success&x=15&y=15, 2007. (accessed December 8, 2008)

Chapter 17:

Cairns W. *About the Size of It: The Common Sense Approach to Measuring Things.* McGraw-Hill Company, MacMillan, 2007.
Senge, P. *The Fifth Discipline.* Currency Press, 2006.
Santa Fe Institute papers on complex adaptive systems are found at
http://www.santafe.edu/. (accessed December 8, 2008)
Baldrige Winners, including corporate profiles and contact information, are available at
http://www.quality.nist.gov/Contacts_Profiles.htm. (accessed December 8, 2008)

Chapter 18:

McGregor, D. *The Human Side of Enterprise.* McGraw-Hill, 2005.
BNET Staff, "Analyzing Your Business's Strengths, Weaknesses, Opportunities, and Threats" available online at http://www.bnet.com/2403-13241_23-53001.html. (accessed December 5, 2008)

Chapter 19:

Boehm, B. and R. Turner. *Balancing Agility and Discipline: A Guide for the Perplexed.* Reading, Massachusetts: Addison-Wesley, 2004.
Cohen, D., M. Lindvall, and P. Costa. "An Introduction to Agile Methods" in *Advances in Computers.* New York: Elsevier Science, 2004.
Gunasekaran, A. *Agile Manufacturing: The 21st Century Competitive Strategy.* New York: Elsevier Science, 2001.
Womack, J. *The Machine That Changed the World: The Story of Lean Production – Toyota's Secret Weapon in the Global Car Wars That Is Now Revolutionizing World Industry.* Free Press, 2007.
"Empowerment in Practice: From Analysis to Implementation."
http://web.worldbank.org/WBSITE/EXTERNAL/TOPICS/EXTPOVERTY/EXTEMPOWE RMENT/0,,contentMDK:20245753~pagePK:210058~piPK:210062~theSitePK:486411,00.html. (accessed December 8, 2008)
"Annual Planning: Strategic Steps That Could Save Your Business."
http://www.nase.org/news/sea/vol11iss2/annual.html. (accessed December 8, 2008)

"25 Companies Where Customers Come First."
http://articles.moneycentral.msn.com/News/25CompaniesWhereCustomersComeFirst.as
px. (accessed December 8, 2008)

Chapter 20:

Buckingham, M., et al. *Now, Discover Your Strengths: How to Develop Your Talents and Those of the People You Manage.* Free Press, 2001.

Dutton, C., et al. *Positive Organizational Scholarship: Foundations of a New Discipline.* San Francisco: Berrett-Koehler, 2004.

Rath, T., et al. *How Full is Your Bucket?* Gallup Press, 2004.

Watson, C. *How Honesty Pays: Restoring Integrity to the Workplace.* Greenwood Publishing Group, Praeger Press, 2005.

Imperato, G..1998. How to give good feedback. *Fast Company,* (August). Available at http://www.fastcompany.com/magazine/17/feedback.html. (accessed December 8, 2008)

"100 Best Companies to Work For." http://www.greatplacetowork.com/best/list-bestusa.htm. (accessed December 8, 2008)

"The 2007 Working Mother 100 Best Companies."
http://www.workingmother.com/web?service=vpage/859. (accessed December 8, 2008)

"Beyond the Balance Sheet—Social Scorecard."
http://www.forbes.com/free_forbes/2004/1213/171tab.html. (accessed December 8, 2008)

End Notes

[i] Sun Tzu. "*Sun Tzu on the Art of War*" Yuni Library.
http://www.yuni.com/library/suntzu.htm#01 (accessed December 3, 2008)

[ii] Cited by: Joe Jenkins, "Humor in Business";
http://www.context.org/ICLIB/IC13/Jenkins.htm (accessed December 3, 2008)

[iii] "The Quotation Page" quotes from Eleanor Roosevelt.
http://www.quotationspage.com/quote/32092.html (accessed December 3, 2008)

[iv] Steve Marr. "Business Proverbs"
http://www.stevemarr.org/index.php?option=com_content&task=view&id=115&Itemid=44
(accessed December 3, 2008)

[v] Think Exist, http://thinkexist.com/quotes/with/keyword/consistency/ (accessed December 8, 2008)

[vi] McCain, John and Marshal Salter, *Why Courage Matters*, (New York: Ballantine Books reprint, 2008)

[vii] "Business Quotes by Dale Carnegie".
http://www.woopidoo.com/business_quotes/authors/dale-carnegie/index.htm (accessed December 3, 2008)

[viii] Discovery Channel. "In Memoriam".
http://dsc.discovery.com/convergence/twintowers/bio/bio2.html (accessed December 3, 2008)

[ix] Kouzes, James M. and Barry Z. Posner. A Leadership Primer based on *The Leadership Challenge*. (New York: John Wiley & Sons, 2007), 68

[x] Professor Allan Cohen, James Watkinson and Jenny Boone, "Herb Kelleher, Executive Chairman of Southwest Airlines Talks about Building Leaders and how their Innovative People-culture has Lifted the Airline to Success" Babson Insights.
http://www.babsoninsight.com/contentmgr/showdetails.php/id/793 (accessed December 3, 2008)

[xi] All Great quotes – Mother Teresa,
http://www.allgreatquotes.com/mother_teresa_quotes.shtml (accessed December 5, 2008)

[xii] "Source of All Knowledge".
http://www.soak.com/topic/leadership/article/tshow/81460/john+adair (accessed December 3, 2008)

[xiii] Performance Magazine Live, "Loyalty Advantage: Increasing Loyalty From Others As The Leader and Towards The Business!", http://performancemagazinelive.com/?page_id=49 (accessed December 3, 2008)

[xiv] Marchi, Jillian. "Leader Biography: Jack Welch", (University of Denver, November 13, 2006)

[xv] Wikipedia on Richard Clark, http://en.wikipedia.org/wiki/Richard_A._Clarke (accessed December 3, 2008)

[xvi] Dr. Michelle Tempest, "The Psychiatrist's Blog", February 21, 2007. http://drmichelletempest.blogspot.com/ (accessed December 3, 2008)

[xvii] Small Business Notes. http://www.smallbusinessnotes.com/planning/mission.html. (accessed December 3, 2008)

[xviii] Tony Mayo. Harvard Business Publishing."The Importance of Vision." October 29, 2007. http://discussionleader.hbsp.com/mayo/2007/10/the_importance_of_vision.html. (accessed December 3, 2008)

[xix] Wisdom Knowledge – Margaret Fuller. http://www.wisdomquotes.com/000615.html (accessed December 5, 2008)

[xx] Brainy Quote Dale Carnegie at http://www.brainyquote.com/quotes/authors/d/dale_carnegie.html (accessed December 5, 2008)

[xxi] Dr. Seuss *One fish two fish red fish blue fish,* (New York: Random House Books for Young Readers March 12, 1960), 50

[xxii] Berkun, Scott. *The Art of Project Management.* O'Reilly Media, Inc. Safari Books Online. 2005.

[xxiii] Susan M. Andersen, Ph. D. and Philip G. Zimbardo, Ph. D., *On Resisting Social Influence,* http://www.icsahome.com/infoserv_articles/andersen_susan_onresistingsocialinfluence_abs.htm (accessed December 3, 2008)

[xxiv] Curios Cat Management Improvement blog http://evop.blogspot.com/2005/10/demings-ideas-at-markeys-audio-visual.html (accessed December 5, 2008)

[xxv] Icelebz quotations from Machiavelli at http://www.icelebz.com/quotes/niccolo_machiavelli/ (accessed December 5, 2008)

[xxvi] Turrentine, T., *"Customer Service: Serving First-Class Lemonade".* http://www.printingsalescoach.com/media_coverage/Customer_Service.pdf.) (accessed December 3, 2008)

[xxvii] *"Leadership Blame and Mistakes";* http://www.nwlink.com/~donclark/leader/blame.html (accessed December 3, 2008)

[xxviii] University of Michigan."The 14 Principles of the Toyota Way." www.si.umich.edu/ICOS/Liker04.pdf. (accessed December 3, 2008)

[xxix] Michalko. Michael. *Tinkertoys* (Berkeley, California: Ten Speed Press; 2 edition (May 15, 2006), 211

[xxx] *Jack Welch Quotes,* http://www.brainyquote.com/quotes/quotes/j/jackwelch130691.html (accessed December 3, 2008)

[xxxi] Ronal Reagan Quotes: http://www.brainyquote.com/quotes/quotes/r/ronaldreag130693.html (accessed December 3, 2008)

xxxii Williamson, Michael. "The Effects of Expanding Employee Decision Making on Contributions to Firm Value in an Informal Reward Environment", University of Texas at Austin - Red McCombs School of Business. http://papers.ssrn.com/sol3/papers.cfm?abstract_id=954349 (accessed December 3, 2008)

xxxiii Army Center for Lessons Learned: http://call.army.mil (accessed December 3, 2008)

xxxiv Wikipedia on disruptive technology: http://en.wikipedia.org/wiki/Disruptive_technology (accessed December 3, 2008)

xxxv (GPRA: *Government Performance and Results Act of 1993, (b) Performance Plans and Reports*, Section 1115. Performance Plans)

xxxvi Quittner, Josh. "The charmed life of Amazon's Jeff Bezos" *Fortune Magazine*, April 15, 2008 available at: http://money.cnn.com/2008/04/14/news/companies/quittner_bezos.fortune/index.htm?postversion=2008041509 (accessed December 8, 2008)

xxxvii Corporate Leadership Council studies are available to members and listed here: https://clc.executiveboard.com/Public/Default.aspx (accessed December 8, 2008)

xxxviii Paul Kedrosky of *The Economist's View* "Wal-mart: Scenes from the Economic Front Lines", October 22, 2008. Available at: http://economistsview.typepad.com/economistsview/2008/10/real-time-wal-m.html. (accessed December 8, 2008)

xxxix Sun Tzu in Wikiquote available at: http://en.wikiquote.org/wiki/Sun_Tzu. (accessed December 8, 2008)

xl C. K. Prahalad, "The Essence of Business Agility," *Information Week*, September 2002.

xli **Spence's basic rules of collaboration:** (Spence, Muneera U. *Graphic Design: Collaborative Processes = Understanding Self and Others*. (lecture) Art 325: Collaborative Processes. Fairbanks Hall, Oregon State University, Corvallis, Oregon. 13 Apr. 2006)

xlii Gallup's Now Discover Your Strengths available at: http://gmj.gallup.com/content/1147/Now-Discover-Your-Strengths-Book-Center.aspx (accessed December 8, 2008)

xliii Gina Imperato, "How to Give Good Feedback". *Fast Company* magazine available at: http://www.fastcompany.com/magazine/17/feedback.html. (accessed December 8, 2008)

Made in the USA
Middletown, DE
25 January 2018